FAITHFUL
IN ALL GOD'S HOUSE
STEWARDSHIP AND THE CHRISTIAN LIFE

FAITHFUL
IN ALL GOD'S HOUSE
STEWARDSHIP AND THE CHRISTIAN LIFE

with a new introduction by Jim Liske

GERARD BERGHOEF

LESTER DEKOSTER

EDITED BY BRETT ELDER

Christian's LIBRARY PRESS

GRAND RAPIDS · MICHIGAN

Christian's Library Press
An imprint of the Acton Institute for the Study of Religion & Liberty
98 E. Fulton
Grand Rapids, Michigan 49503
www.clpress.com

Cover and interior design by Sharon VanLoozenoord
Editing by Brett Elder, Timothy J. Beals, and Elizabeth Banks

21 20 19 18 17 16 15 14 13 1 2 3 4 5 6 7 8 9 10

Printed in the United States of America
Second edition

CONTENTS

INTRODUCTION

You and I have been created in the image of God. Have you ever really considered the ramifications of that truth? God has woven into us threads of his creativity, authority, compassion, emotion, intelligence, justice, and more. In creation, God poured his essence into us.

Stewardship is the primary human activity that reveals God's image within us. Stewardship is an activity that leads us to an identity. We do what God wants us to do *so that* we can become who he wants us to be. With incredible grace, our Heavenly Father is always doing something in us, with us, and through us. As we journey with him, using his gifts according to his intentions, he changes us and the world around us to more perfectly reflect his grace, justice, and truth.

I love the New Testament word that we translate as "stewardship." In the original Greek, the word is *oikonomia*. From that Greek word we get English phrases like "specific economy" and "administration of household or estate." The word translated "steward" is *oikonomos*. From that word, we derive "overseer," "treasurer," and "distributor." From those terms and how they are used throughout the New Testament, we can understand a biblical steward as one who "manages a house for an owner" or one who "tends to the economy that another has supplied." Quite simply, we have been given the awesome task of keeping God's house—his creation—in order.

In *Faithful in All God's House*, Lester DeKoster and Gerard Berghoef further define stewardship as "willed acts of service that, not only make and sustain the fabric of civilization and culture, but also develop the soul." The authors contend that "while the object of work is destined to perish, the soul formed by daily decision to do work carries over into eternity." The eternal image of God blossoms inside us as we go about his business. As we allow God to use us to change the world, he is quietly but continually conforming us to his likeness.

DeKoster and Berghoef artfully set stewardship forward as a gift from God to us. He has charged us with the awesome responsibility to care for and manage the world he lovingly set in motion. The power and authority to fulfill our divine appointment flow from God's ownership and sovereignty over all things; however, as the authors recognize, sin often prevents us from meeting the demands of stewardship. Only the grace of God—demonstrated in Jesus' atoning act—restores us to the position we forfeited. Through Christ, we once again become agents of God's redemptive plan. What was lost in the Fall has been regained through the work of God's Son on the cross. Now, as followers of Jesus and stewards of all he has made, we marvel as his Kingdom is daily revealed in and through us.

One other foundational truth about biblical stewardship is emphasized in *Faithfulness in All God's House*: We are not God's employees or slaves—we are his partners, like beloved children apprenticed in the family business we will one day inherit. God invites us to join him in the mission of revealing his righteousness to a watching world. Biblical stewardship is an exciting calling, one that makes everything we do an opportunity to collaborate with God. As we serve him and he reveals his image within us, his compassion for those around us actually wells up in our hearts, and we are privileged to express it. As he grants us the ability to remain committed, our lives overflow with joyful, awestruck celebration of what God has given to us and—through us—to others.

Life offers us many conflicting standards of success and fulfillment that loudly vie for our attention. If we are not intentional about allowing God's image to emerge from us more and more, these competing priorities will confuse and mislead us, eventually crippling our ability to minister to the world around us. By contrast, a life of biblical stewardship brings purpose and clarity to our lives and to our ministry. As we follow Jesus day by day, we will more readily recognize his voice, and we will join him in bringing love, hope, and peace to his world. God is bringing redemption to all of creation, and he has invited us—his stewards—to bring that about with him.

That's an invitation I want to accept, and I hope you will, too.

Jim Liske
CEO, Prison Fellowship Ministries
Lansdowne, Virginia

THE FORMS OF STEWARDSHIP 1

Stewardship is far more than the handling of our money. Stewardship is the handling of life, and time, and destiny.

Money does indeed do many things. Using our money as good stewards is certainly one of the severest tests of our citizenship in his kingdom. However, stewardship extends beyond giving money.

THE COMMON FORMS

The forms which stewardship assumes are defined, first of all, by the human needs we encounter. And the needs we meet are the needs that we in fact become aware of. Be assured that God provides a need, within reach, for every talent, every skill, and every gift of any kind that he gives us. It is simply hardness of heart that blinds the eye, closes the ear, and lames the limbs when opportunities for good stewardship are unobserved.

Like the pussy cat who went to London, in the fable, for to see the queen, but who saw only a mouse beneath her throne, so we perceive in the world about us—beginning at home—only what we have the heart bent on encountering. A heart softened by grace and beating, now, in tune with divine love finds opportunities for stewardship in direct proportion to the gifts that God has given for that purpose. Gift and need are divinely matched. The need may, in fact, alert us to gifts we did not know we had.

The basic forms of stewardship are twice defined: (1) by the opportunities for doing good that we learn to become aware of, and (2) by the gifts God has on deposit with us designed to meet such opportunities.

The Bible puts the basic forms of stewardship within everyone's reach by speaking in terms of cups of cold water, going an extra mile, crusts of bread, a helping hand, the exercise of patience, and the like. Make a list sometime of the very ordinary forms of stewardship the Bible asks of us. It will become clear that basic stewardship is concerned with sweetening human relationships in our everyday world. Nothing momentous. Something like a genuine smile, nod, wave, kindly word, the steadying hand; and the sensitive heart, compassionate spirit, flowing out into acts of kindness, generosity, trust, and grace. Time invested in these virtues is time invested in heaven. None is beyond our reach—if the heart is aware, and the will bent to do God's service wherever and whenever . . . .

SPECIAL FORMS

Some aspects of stewardship are defined by the extent of the gifts God entrusts to us.

Has he given you wealth? Steward it in service of the needy, both in kind and by way of the influence which wealth gives.

Has he given you position? Fill it gracefully and for the good of all those whose lives you affect.

Has he given you talents of various kinds? Use yours for the benefit of the community. Whatever the uncommon gift, it is given to serve. So steward it.

WORK

The basic form of stewardship is daily work. No matter what that work may be.

No matter if you have never before looked on your job as other than a drudge, a bore, or a fearful trial. Know that the harder it is for you to face each working day, the more your will to persevere schools the soul.

Work is the fundamental form of stewardship because:

God himself works: "My Father is always at his work to this very day, and I, too, am working" (John 5:17), the Lord says. It is not recounted that God plays, but he works. That is to say, God is ever-busy making provision for our existence. Work is that which serves another. Play is that which serves ourselves. *Work knits the fabric of civilization.* We take for granted all the possibilities which work alone provides. And we become aware of how work sustains the order which makes life possible when that order is rent by lightning flashes of riot or war, and the necessities which work normally provides become difficult to come by. *Man's history begins in a garden and mounts to a city.* A garden is what God the Holy Spirit does, without man, with a wilderness. A city is what God the Holy Spirit does through man's work. *It is of the nature of work to serve the community.* Whether work is done in the home, on the land, or in the countless forms of enterprise developed across the centuries, work is doubly blessed: (1) it provides for the family of man, and (2) it matures the worker. *Work matures the worker because it requires ethical decision.* Merely to rise to one's daily tasks requires an act of will, a decision to serve the community, however reluctantly, however unaware the worker may be that such is the case. Such willed acts of service not only make and sustain the fabric of civilization and culture, but also develop the soul. And, while the object of work is destined to perish, the soul formed by daily decision to do work carries over into eternity.

This perspective on work, as a maturing of the soul, liberates the believer from undue concern over the monotony of the assembly line, the threat of technology, or the reduction of the worker to but an easily replaceable cog in the industrial machine. One's job may be done by another. But each doer is himself unique, and what carries over beyond life and time is not the work but the worker. What doing the job does for each of us is not repeated in anyone else. What the exercise of will, of tenacity, of courage, of foresight, of triumph over temptations to get by, does for you is uniquely your own. One worker may replace another on the assembly line, but what each worker carries away from meeting the challenge of doing the day's shift will ever be his own. The lasting and creative consequence of daily work happens to the worker. God so arranges that civilization grows out of the same effort that develops the soul.

The forms of work are countless, but the typical one is work with the hands. The Bible has reference to the sower, to the making of tents and of things out of clay, to tilling the fields and tending the vine. Handwork makes visible the plan in the mind, just as the deed makes visible the love in the heart. While the classic Greek mind tended to scorn work with the hands, the Bible suggests that something about it structures the soul.

The results of one's work can never be fully known. What will become of the produce raised, of the machine built, of the person fed? No one can foretell what will be the final consequence of today's effort. Nor does the paycheck really measure the value, nor the effort, of the work for which it is given. Wages are set by the market, and the results of work are hidden in the mists of tomorrow. What endures is what happens to the worker who bravely makes it through the day.

Seen in this light, which is the light shed by the Bible on work, it is easy to understand why work is the primary form of stewardship. To work, most of us give the largest unit of our lives. By work, we together raise the level of our culture, keep its order, supply its needs, and point to its promise of better living for more of the world's peoples.

For the believer; then, stewardship begins with the day's work. Done well, as unto God, in the full knowledge that by work the world lives, work serves God and man and the self.

PLAY

We have spoken of play as that which is done to please or serve the self. Play may absorb much effort, long planning, and lots of time. But so long as the end in view is the satisfaction of the self, such effort cannot be called work. This is true whatever the form of play, whatever its esteem in the community as compared with work. What the self heaps up in time for its own use does not carry over into eternity, and burdens the soul that is thus occupied.

Play may be indulged as recreation, that is, as preparation for doing work better when the worker has been so refreshed.

You will know whether it is work, or play, which is occupying your time, your effort, and . . . your life. And knowing, you can yourself judge whether the time and effort you give to any activity is work, an investment in eternity, or play, and an investment in temporality.

THE FUNDAMENTALS   2
OF STEWARDSHIP

The practice of stewardship is the supreme challenge of the Christian life. The Bible makes stewardship the key to Christian behavior.

THE STEWARD

Who is a steward? What is a steward?

Eliezer was steward over the vast household of Abraham. That is to say, Eliezer was in charge of all that Abraham had (Gen. 24:1).

Joseph was steward of the household of Potiphar, officer of Pharoah, who "put him in charge of his household, and he entrusted to his care everything he owned" (Gen. 39:4).

The steward owns nothing and governs everything. To him, the master commits control of all that he possesses—all, that is, of the master's material goods. This high and responsible office, mentioned in the first book of the Old Testament and in the first and third books of the New Testament in the parables of Jesus: "There was a rich man whose manager . . ." (Luke 16:1); "When evening came, the owner of the vineyard said to his foreman . . ." (Matt. 20:8).

Later in the New Testament, Paul writes of his own calling, "Now it is required that those who have been given a trust must prove faithful" (1 Cor. 4:2). Peter applies the concept of stewardship to the Christian life, saying: "Each one should use whatever gift he has received to serve others, faithfully administering God's grace in its various forms. If anyone speaks, he should do it as one speaking the very words of God. If anyone serves, he should do it with the strength God provides, so that in all things God may be praised through Jesus Christ" (1 Peter 4:10–11).

The parables of the talents (Matt. 25:14–30) and of the minas (Luke 19:11–27) show that the steward will be required to render account of all that has been placed under his stewardship.

God makes man steward of his world. Who is man, asks the psalmist? He answers: "You made him a little lower than the heavenly beings and crowned him with glory and honor. You made him ruler over the works of your hands; you put everything under his feet" (Ps. 8:5–6).

God makes man the master of his temporal household. Like all stewards, man is not the owner. He is the overseer. For three score years and ten, more or less as the case may be, each of us is steward over those talents and those pounds allotted us by divine providence. At the end comes the accounting: "After a long time the master of those servants returned and settled accounts with them" (Matt. 25:19). "He was made king, however, and returned home. Then he sent for the servants to whom he had given the money, in order to find out what they had gained with it" (Luke 19:15).

As each has managed his stewardship, so will he be judged: "Well done, my good servant!" or, "But those enemies of mine who did not want me to be king over them—bring them here and kill them in front of me" (Luke 19:17, 27). The quality of stewardship depends on obedience to the Master's will. The steward who does not obey the Master's law rejects the Master's authority and serves another. Our stewardship is the test: Do we mean to serve God or mammon, the Lord or the Devil?

Stewardship is, we repeat, key to the Christian life—and death, and judgment.

BASIC PRINCIPLES OF STEWARDSHIP

The fundamentals of stewardship as revealed in Scripture are briefly stated:

All things are made and sustained by God: "In the beginning God created the heavens and the earth" (Gen. 1:1). "The earth is the LORD's, and everything in it, the world, and all who live in it" (Ps. 24:1). Moses says: "To the LORD your God belong the heavens, even the highest heavens, the earth and everything in it" (Deut. 10:14). All is God's, including man himself. This is the first and most basic fundamental of stewardship. It is a truth of revelation that we must never forget.

God gives and sustains human life, as he sets man within his world: "The LORD God formed the man from the dust of the ground and breathed into his nostrils the breath of life, and the man became a living being" (Gen. 2:7). "In his hand is the life of every creature and the breath of all mankind" (Job 12:10). God gives us life, and time, and a world in which to live it. Still, all is from him: Christians, remember.

God decides when to terminate the life he gives: "You turn men back to dust, saying, 'Return to dust, O sons of men'" (Ps. 90:3). God sustains all the moments between birth and death: "My times are in your hands" (Ps. 31:15).

God determines the distribution of goods received by each during his lifetime: "The LORD sends poverty and wealth; he humbles and he exalts" (1 Sam. 2:7). What each of us has to steward, what each receives as talent or pound, is wholly from God. Everyone believes that whatever he owns has been acquired by the sweat of his own brow or the shrewdness of his own wit. This is not what Scripture teaches: "You may say to yourself, 'My power and the strength of my hands have produced this wealth for me.' But remember the LORD your God, for it is he who gives you the ability to produce wealth, and so confirms his covenant, which he swore to your forefathers, as it is today" (Deut. 8:17). There are no self-made men; there are only God-made men. All that we have is his gift. "The blessing of the LORD brings wealth" (Prov. 10:22). The steward must first of all know whose goods they are that he administers and recognize that whatever he has in his hands comes to him from the master. Not to know this is to risk idolatry, as the prophet says to Israel: "She has not acknowledged that I was the one who gave her the grain, the new wine and oil, who lavished on her the silver and gold—which they used for Baal" (Hos. 2:8). It is pagan to think that things come by chance. It is self-idolatry to think that possessions come by our own earning. It is Christian to know that all we have comes as a gift from God. This knowledge, too, is basic to a right understanding of stewardship. Indeed, if we owned that which we are called to steward, we would no longer be stewards but masters.

Because he is creator, owner, and master of all, God alone sets the requirements for stewardship of his goods and of the world. Between himself and those who would be his faithful stewards, God makes a covenant: "Obey me and do everything I command you, and you will be my people, and I will be your God" (Jer. 11:4).

The revealed law governing stewardship comes to expression in the Ten Commandments. The meaning of the Commandments is expounded by the prophets. It is repeated by Jesus Christ, and applied by the apostles. The whole Bible is the book of this covenant: "So in everything, do to others what you would have them do to you, for this sums up the Law and the Prophets" (Matt. 7:12). Every steward chooses one of two ways: "Enter through the narrow gate. For wide is the gate and broad is the road that leads to destruction, and many enter through it. But small is the gate and narrow the road that leads to life, and only a few find it" (Matt. 7:13–14).

However, both ways come to judgment: "And I saw the dead, great and small, standing before the throne, and books were opened. Another book was opened, which is the book of life. The dead were judged according to what they had done as recorded in the books" (Rev. 20:12). The Bible opens with the days of creation and ends with the Day of Judgment. Between them lies, for every person, the period of stewardship when God makes each person responsible for the use of his gifts according to his directions. These are the fundamentals of the doctrine of stewardship. They explain why stewardship is key to the Christian life.

Let us summarize the basics of stewardship:

1. God creates, sustains, and thus owns all things—man included. Not only in the beginning, but always. Every child born into the world receives life from God.
2. God brings us to life within this vast, beautiful, and challenging world and permits us to use and enjoy all that he sustains.
3. He intends, however, that his will shall govern our wills and his desires shall control our desires. He reveals his will in inspired Scripture. As we walk in his world, his word is a lamp to our feet and a light for our paths (Ps. 119:105).

4. Our use of God's property, whether as faithful or rebellious stewards, is, therefore, what life is all about.
5. Our obedience, or disobedience, to God's will revealed in his Word becomes the basis for the last judgment, which is the prelude to heaven or hell.

DIFFICULTIES

Creation

The basic tenets of stewardship can give rise to problems and objections that believers may meet. We discuss some of those problems and objections here.

The doctrine of creation is, of course, challenged by the theory of evolution. This theory is now advocated with far less assurance than once it was, but it still sets the secular trend. Christians cannot hope to demonstrate the truth of creationism before they act on the truth of stewardship. Without engaging in endless dispute, the believer wisely relies on faith as found in Scripture. God is creator. Man is his creation. Whether or not the biblical account permits an interpretation that allows for long periods of time in the process of creation, the crux of the issue is that *God made all that is*; that he made man in his own image; and that man, made perfect, chose to disobey and fall into sin. All this is revelation; all else is speculation. It is far better to take the Word at what it says than to lose the truth and clarity of Genesis in the maze of shifting science.

Do not be misled, either, by secular deprecations of the earth as being but a tiny speck of dust that is lost in an immense universe. Remember that Genesis teaches that God spoke the universe into being. When the infinite and majestic God speaks, he says much. Small wonder that the glories of the starry skies stretch far beyond our comprehension. Are you surprised that galaxies and universes begin when God speaks? Leave it to those who have no faith to belittle man in comparison with the stars that were made expressly for man's delight. Recall that of all created things only man is made in God's image: "For in the image of God has God made man" (Gen. 9:6). About the stars God says: "Lift your eyes and look to the heavens: Who created all these? He who brings out the starry host one by one, and calls them each by name. Because of

his great power and mighty strength, not one of them is missing"
(Isa. 40:26). The prophet Isaiah says the wonder of the heavens
excite our confidence in the Creator, for "the LORD is the everlast-
ing God, the Creator of the ends of the earth. He will not grow
tired or weary, and his understanding no one can fathom. He
gives strength to the weary and increases the power of the weak"
(Isa. 40:28–29). The unending vastness, the throbbing energy, the
sparkling fire, the utter mystery of space is meant to awaken us to
God whose image we bear and on whose strength we can depend.

In making his universe, God laid down patterns of behavior
for it. We call these patterns "natural law." Do not let natural law
intrude between you and the active presence of God all about us.
"My Father is always at his work," our Lord says, "and I, too, am
working" (John 5:17). We also call this working natural law. God,
not meteorology, sends the weather. God gives the leaves, awak-
ens the sun, rides on the storm: "He says to the snow, 'Fall on the
earth,' and to the rain shower, 'Be a mighty downpour.' The breath
of God produces ice, and the broad waters become frozen. He loads
the clouds with moisture; he scatters his lightning through them.
At his direction they swirl around over the face of the whole earth
to do whatever he commands them" (Job 37:6, 10–12).

The doctrine of stewardship is impressed on us by a vivid sense
of God's immanent activity in all that we often take for granted or
account as natural behavior.

Life

None chooses to be born because that is a decision made before
birth. We did not ask for life; God gives it to us. Nowadays medicine employs all that is now known of natural law to prolong life
against disease, but God numbers our days: "Man's days are determined; you have decreed the number of his months and have
set limits he cannot exceed" (Job 14:5). The time for the tests of
stewardship is not ours to measure, nor enlarge: "Who of you by
worrying can add a single hour to his life?" (Matt. 6:27). The
hoarding of goods that competes with stewardship has its roots in
anxiety about the morrow—an anxiety our Lord rejects because
our tomorrows are in God's hand. The time and place of our
birth, our family, our race, our talents, our looks—are all by God's
design. Some are born to wealth; others see the light of day in the

clutch of destitution. Where and how life is given is God's choice and our lot. Neither envy of the rich nor scorn for the poor befits our heritage, for where we were born was not of our choosing—and the envy or scorn falls on him who made us.

Freedom

God holds us responsible for our stewardship because he has made us free. Thus, freedom cannot be harmonized with natural law. We are not patterned, as are the stars and the atoms, by a divine activity so consistent that we speak of it as law. God respects the liberty of his image bearers. God does not invade the human spirit. Demons take possession if they can; "Here I am! I stand at the door and knock" (Rev. 3:20). With infinite delicacy, the Creator respects the integrity of the man he has made. This cannot be explained because a freedom explained is not freedom, for explanation involves cause and effect. Freedom has no cause; it is a divine gift.

However, the atoms of our bodies obey natural law. This is the foundation of medicine. Yet the self, intertwined with the flesh of the body, is free, and because it is free, it is therefore responsible for the stewardship it exercises. This we do not explain; this we affirm: Every command in Scripture assumes freedom.

The mystery of freedom is further complicated by the "secret power of lawlessness" (2 Thess. 2:7). How sin entered God's good creation is told to us in Genesis (chapter 3). However, there is no explanation for sin. As a sinner, man lost an aspect of his freedom. No longer, after the defection of Adam, could man obey the law of stewardship simply through his own choice: "As it is written: 'There is no one righteous, not even one; there is no one who understands, no one who seeks God. All have turned away, they have together become worthless; there is no one who does good, not even one'" (Rom. 3:10–12).

What fallen man, then, could not do for himself—properly use God's goods—Jesus Christ makes possible for us. He died for our sins that in him "we too may live a new life" (Rom. 6:4). This newness is manifest in stewardship—that is, in what the Bible calls good works: "For we are God's workmanship, created in Christ Jesus to do good works, which God prepared in advance for us to do" (Eph. 2:10). Stewardship, freely chosen in accord with God's law, is possible in Christ Jesus. Our works do not save us (Rom. 3:28), but rather we are saved for good works—that is, for stewardship.

Getting the Word

How shall the law go forth? How shall mankind hear the demand for stewardship? Through the church. God lays upon the church the responsibility for stewardship education: "Therefore go and make disciples of all nations, baptizing them in the name of the Father and of the Son and of the Holy Spirit, and teaching them to obey everything I have commanded you" (Matt. 28:19–20). Observe from this passage, commonly called the Great Commission:

> The mandate is given to the apostles, founders of the New Testament church. Through them the church is required to disciple all nations; a disciple being one who follows the teaching of a master. Believers are to be Christ's disciples, taken into the church by baptism.
> The church is commanded to teach disciples to do all that the Lord has commanded; that is, teach all believers his application and interpretation of the law and the prophets—in other words, the governing principles of stewardship.
> The primary task of the church, then, is to proclaim the Word that generates new birth and to teach the Word that governs the life of stewardship.

Obviously, Christian stewardship will be most successfully practiced whenever and wherever the church most obediently is the church.

What Life Is All About

The meaning of life is the subject of endless speculation and confusion among those who fail to seek life's purpose from the giver of life. Those looking for light on life from words other than the Word of God can find countless books, articles, lectures, study groups, exotic religions, and gurus and so-called masters crying out to confuse them. Only God knows why he gives us life, the time to use life, and all his gifts, as well as the talents to employ them aright. God tells us in Scripture and through the church, which he sustains for teaching mankind, what life is all about.

Life and time are God's primary gifts. To live is to have time. To have time is to live. Time enshrines what we do with life. There is no doing over. The past is past. That which our doing pours into the mold of time is what life is all about. Our doing serves God or mammon— the Lord's word or the devil's lie. This is the crucial choice for which time gives life opportunity: "Choose for yourselves this day whom you will serve" (Josh. 24:15). Time always registers today and is opportunity and obligation: "Encourage one another daily, as long as it is called Today, so that none of you may be hardened by sin's deceitfulness" (Heb. 3:13). Jesus said, "As long as it is day, we must do the work of him who sent me. Night is coming, when no one can work" (John 9:4).

To live is to be confronted by choice. Choice leads to doing. Time crystallizes deed in anticipation of the judgment. Life is the God-given power to use the God-given gift of time in obedience to the giver. Faith is the God-given power to obey the Word instead of self-interests or the words of unbelief: "Choose for yourselves this day" for it is always today until the night comes.

Judgment

If salvation is by faith, the free gift of God, why then is there a final judgment? "For God will bring every deed into judgment, including every hidden thing, whether it is good or evil" (Eccl. 12:14). "The dead were judged according to what they had done as recorded in the books" (Rev. 20:12). "God will give to each person according to what he has done" (Rom. 2:6). How can this be if salvation is not by works but by faith: "For it is by grace you have been saved, through faith—and this not from yourselves, it is the gift of God—not by works, so that no one can boast" (Eph. 2:8–9)?

Every believer knows, in the depths of his heart, that he can no more earn heaven than he can climb the sky to reach it. Therefore, we are not surprised that the Bible rejects the notion that salvation is the reward for good works. For what, then, are believers to be judged? It is undeniable that judgment on our works does await us. Texts affirming that, such as those already quoted, could be multiplied. However, an answer to this difficulty is suggested by the miracles of Jesus. He made the blind to see, the deaf to hear, the lame to walk. He even made the dead alive again.

Why did he do all this? Sometimes he did it to validate the Lord's call for belief in him (see John 20:30–31), but he also did it for another reason: to restore these crippled organs to use so that even the dead-made-alive could put the gift of life to use once more. That which once stood in the way of normal life was removed. The sick and the deformed and the demon- possessed were liberated by a word from the Lord.

In the same way, the believer is today liberated by the same word, through faith, from what stands in the way of a new life of obedience.

Take note of these things about faith and the resulting miracles (1) A miracle is not an end in itself. Often it is followed by the Lord's parting admonition: Go, do. A handicap is gone. A life is restored. What then? How will the new freedom be used? The question then is the question now. (2) The Lord's miracle of healing usually came in response to faith: "Your faith has healed you" (Matt. 9:22). "'If you can?' said Jesus. 'Everything is possible for him who believes'" (Mark 9:23). Faith is the road that miracles walk; faith is the vehicle on which miracles ride—no less today than when Jesus walked the earth. (3) Faith is the means to wholeness. Faith accepts newness of life. Faith enters after one is liberated in Christ Jesus. The new life, given through faith, reveals its presence in good works: "His faith was made complete by what he did" (James 2:22). The purpose of healing finds its goal in the obedient use of the body made new. (4) The miraculous restoration or liberation of life through faith goes on now in every believer. A life dead in sin is raised to newness in obedience. Eyes blind to the presence of God in creation (Ps. 19:1) and to the presence of Christ in the needy see once again. Ears deaf to the Word and to the cries of the oppressed hear and provoke a response. Limbs lamed by self- indulgence are extended to serve a neighbor. All these examples are evidence that faith is indeed present; without these faith is dead: "Faith by itself, if it is not accompanied by action, is dead" (James 2:17). (5) Decisions regarding the Final Judgment, being focused on works, are made on the presence or absence of faith. By faith we are saved (Eph. 2:8), and faith is revealed by our works. Without faith we are lost, as revealed by our works: "The dead were judged according to what they had done" (Rev. 20:12).

WHAT MAY I KEEP   3
FOR MYSELF?

How much of my goods, time, interests, and talents do I owe the needy? Or, how much of all that God gives me may I keep for myself? How does anyone answer such questions? First, by putting them to the Scriptures; second, by setting the scriptural answers into his own time and place.

THE SCRIPTURES

The Bible never gives a dollars-and-cents answer to questions such as these. The Bible functions through the conscience, and to sensitize conscience, the Bible does suggest an investor's guide that the pulpit should be urged to apply frequently to the congregation. The prudent believer will apply it to himself and assist others in applying it to themselves.

An investor's guide is simply this: Give to the needy all the goods, time, talent, and effort that you want to invest in heaven. Give to the needy whatever you want to reap beyond the grave. Keep for yourself whatever you do not want to see again in any form after your eyelids close for the last time. The Bible thus serves as an investor's manual. The prudent investor takes heed. This is what the Lord teaches through his remarks to the rich young ruler: "Go, sell everything you have and give to the poor, and you will have treasure in heaven" (Mark 10:21). The Lord thus confirms the inspired teaching of Proverbs: "He who is kind to the poor lends to the LORD, and he will reward him for what he has done" (Prov. 19:17).

Paul compares heavenly investment with sowing seed that comes to fruition in eternity: "Whoever sows sparingly will also reap sparingly, and whoever sows generously will also reap generously" (2 Cor. 9:6). A stingy planting guarantees a poor harvest. Believers must take the significance of this language of sowing and reaping very seriously. God does. The Spirit inspires the apostle to say very plainly: "Do not be deceived: God cannot be mocked. A man reaps what he sows" (Gal. 6:7). Lending to the Lord by way of giving to the poor is secure investment. It survives even death itself. It is, moreover, gilt-edged and blue chip: "Give, and it will be given to you. A good measure, pressed down, shaken together and running over, will be poured into your lap. For with the measure you use, it will be measured to you," says the Lord Jesus (Luke 6:38). Jesus states in Mark 4:24: "'Consider carefully what you hear,' he continued. 'With the measure you use, it will be measured to you—and even more.'" This is also why Paul molds the conscience in these words: "It is more blessed to give than to receive" (Acts 20:35)—a saying he attributes to Jesus.

It is in this light that we all must understand the warnings in the Bible against riches (for details see chapter 12). We must view wealth and the pursuit of wealth with a very wary eye. The Lord calls him a *fool* whose heart is set solely on personal gain, and he tells a now familiar parable to illustrate the warning.

> The ground of a certain rich man produced a good crop. He thought to himself, "What shall I do? I have no place to store my crops."
>
> Then he said, "This is what I'll do. I will tear down my barns and build bigger ones, and there I will store all my grain and my goods. And I'll say to myself, 'You have plenty of good things laid up for many years. Take life easy; eat, drink and be merry.'"
>
> But God said to him, "You fool! This very night your life will be demanded from you. Then who will get what you have prepared for yourself?"
>
> "This is how it will be with anyone who stores up things for himself but is not rich toward God." (Luke 12:16–21)

This illustrates how one becomes "rich toward God"—give to the poor.

"How hard it is," Jesus says, "for the rich to enter the kingdom of God!" That is, how hard it is for the rich to obey God's command-ments—for only they who are truly citizens of the kingdom obey its laws in obedience to its king. Indeed, the Lord goes on to say, "It is easier for a camel to go through the eye of a needle than for a rich man to enter the kingdom of God" (Mark 10:23, 25). "Now listen, you rich people," James writes, "weep and wail because of the misery that is coming upon you" (James 5:1). The day of accounting is com-ing. Those who have made no investments beyond that judgment day do well to weep and wail and quickly amend their selfish ways.

Are warnings like these preached from your pulpit? Urgently and often? Or does someone try to blunt their edge by saying that salvation is only by grace? Beware of this fatal mistake.

Of course, salvation is God's gift, out of his sheer grace—this is the teaching of the whole Bible, and grace is free. Those who have truly received this free grace are made investors in heaven through deeds of love: "What good is it, my brothers, if a man claims to have faith but has no deeds? Can such faith save him? Suppose a brother or sister is without clothes and daily food. If one of you says to him, 'Go, I wish you well; keep warm and well fed,' but does nothing about his physical needs, what good is it? In the same way, faith by itself, if it is not accompanied by ac-tion, is dead" (James 2:14–17). Grace, received through faith, does not ease the obligation to invest in heaven through gifts to the needy. Against the pull of self-interest and the excuses of selfish-ness, grace makes such investment possible.

Does this mean that I give to the needy out of my life—time, concern, talents, and goods that God has given me? The Bible's answer is clear: Give whatever you want to invest beyond the grave. Keep whatever you hope never to see again. This is the clear teaching of the Scripture—God's investment manual.

PRACTICAL APPLICATION

The church functions where the love of money and the love of God meet—and clash. Everyone is likely to feel the tensions of that conflict.

It will be pointed out, perhaps, that in fact the Bible mentions with divine approval certain very rich men. Abraham, the father of the faithful (Rom. 4:16): "Abram had become very wealthy in livestock and in silver and gold" (Gen. 13:2). So was Joseph of Arimathea, whose riches gave him access to Pilate, the Roman governor of Israel (Matt. 27:57–58). While it is true that the rich young ruler was asked to "sell everything . . . and give to the poor" (Mark 10:21), it is also true that wealthy Zacchaeus was blessed when he gave half of his possessions to the poor (Luke 19:8–10).

What practical instruction may be derived from these and similar biblical examples? The rich who win God's favor are generous to the needy. Job was rich and received God's final blessing after many trials. He speaks for the biblical wealthy who enjoyed God's favor: I rescued the poor who cried for help, and the fatherless who had none to assist him. The man who was dying blessed me; I made the widow's heart sing. I put on righteousness as my clothing; justice was my robe and my turban. I was eyes to the blind and feet to the lame. I was a father to the needy; I took up the case of the stranger. I broke the fangs of the wicked and snatched the victims from their teeth (Job 29:12–17).

The rich who received God's blessing made double use of their wealth.

They ministered directly to the needy. They also used the power entrusted them by their God-given wealth to rescue the defenseless from the clutches of the unrighteous ("I broke the fangs of the wicked and snatched the victims from their teeth," says Job). So used, the riches kept after generous giving to the needy ("I give half of my possessions to the poor") attain the purpose for which God gives them.

It is not money in itself but the *love* of money that is evil. Paul sums up to Timothy the verdict of his own experience in these words: "For the love of money is a root of all kinds of evil. Some people, eager for money, have wandered from the faith and pierced themselves with many griefs" (1 Tim. 6:10). Paul thus repeats the teaching of our Lord in the parable of the sower: "The one who received the seed that fell among the thorns is the man who hears the word, but the worries of this life and the deceitfulness of wealth choke it, making it unfruitful" (Matt. 13:22). Wealth and power may bear no fruit regarding the needy and the oppressed. Why not? Because the love that should focus on the poor is turned inward to the possession of wealth and the enjoyments it seems to provide. Such love of money is condemned.

Joseph of Arimathea was able to ask for the body of Jesus from Pontius Pilate. No doubt he found Pilate's door open to him because he was rich; not everyone had immediate access to Pilate's office. What is at stake is whether these doors are opened in the service of Jesus or of self. Is the rich man's influence exerted for the common good or for his own? Is the influential word he might speak silenced by self-interest, or is it spoken from the rooftops for the benefit of justice? God gives wealth to whom he will. Wealth not only can provide goods to supply the wants of the needy, but it is also power. The Bible does not require that every believer give all his money away. Why not? Because God has uses for the power of wealth committed to justice. It is the task of the church to alert the rich to this supreme obligation.

There remains, though, the nagging question: What, then, may anyone keep for himself? The answer, which must finally be measured by each in the light of Word and of conscience as schooled by the church, is to *keep whatever I truly need for my calling.* Because God allots each human a task and whatever wealth is required to effectively do that task is ours to keep. Indeed, charity is God's way of providing the needy with the essentials of life requisite to their own callings. No one can decide for another precisely what he may keep for himself. God's Word and the church must teach this vitally important question. God will, at the last day, pass judgment on how much his gifts were used in his service.

It is easy to understand why the Bible warns so soberly and so frequently and so vividly against the "deceitfulness of riches." We are easily beguiled into thinking that our wealth is our own; that *we* have *earned* "every penny" of it; that those who have less must be lazy or spendthrift; and that God signals our special virtue by giving us special blessings. All the while the Word is warning against just such self-deception.

In short, God's gifts of life, time, talent, possessions, and skills are realized as blessings when used to sustain us in *our* callings, to support the needy in *their* callings, *and* to get justice done among men to the fullest extent of our ability and power. These gifts, however, become a curse when exclusively abused for our own selfish designs. "Just as man is destined to die once, and after that to face judgment" (Heb. 9:27). It is with an eye on this solemn guarantee that the church *must*, however difficult it may be, work diligently in doing what it can to alert every member to the obligations imposed by his riches. God's warning to Ezekiel passes to us:

> Son of man, I have made you a watchman for the house of Israel; so hear the word I speak and give them warning from me. When I say to a wicked man, "You will surely die," and you do not warn him or speak out to dissuade him from his evil ways in order to save his life, that wicked man will die for his sin, and I will hold you accountable for his blood. But if you do warn the wicked man and he does not turn from his wickedness or from his evil ways, he will die for his sin; but you will have saved yourself.
>
> Again, when a righteous man turns from his righteousness and does evil, and I put a stumbling block before him, he will die. Since you did not warn him, he will die for his sin. The righteous things he did will not be remembered, and I will hold you accountable for his blood. But if you do warn the righteous man not to sin and he does not sin, he will surely live because he took warning, and you will have saved yourself. (Ezek. 3:17–21)

Stewarding is a sober business. Pray fervently and often that God will qualify you for doing it well.

Why should Christians give? The Bible clearly teaches that giving is not optional. Why? Love gives. Giving is the natural expression of love. "God is love" (1 John 4:16); "For God so loved the world that he gave his one and only Son" (John 3:16). Love gives. Jesus equates love with giving: "Greater love has no one than this, that he lay down his life for his friends" (John 15:13). Love compels giving; indeed love is giving—so much so that refusal to give betrays the absence of love: "If anyone has material possessions and sees his brother in need but has no pity on him, how can the love of God be in him?" (1 John 3:17).

Paul also defines the willingness to give as evidence of love: "Therefore show these men the proof of your love" (2 Cor. 8:24). This after he has boasted of the love shown through liberality by the churches of Macedonia "that they gave as much as they were able, and even beyond their ability" (2 Cor. 8:3). Giving, then, flows from love. To love is to give. Not to give is not to love.

Love is mandatory. "Live a life of love, just as Christ loved us and gave himself up for us" (Eph. 5:2). "And he has given us this command: Whoever loves God must also love his brother" (1 John 4:21). "Love the Lord your God with all your heart and with all your soul and with all your mind." This is the first and greatest commandment. And the second is like it: "Love your neighbor as yourself." All the Law and the Prophets hang on these two commandments" (Matt. 22:37–40). Love is mandatory. What shall we give to God to show our love? Obedience. What shall we give to our neighbors to show our love? A generous share of the gifts God has given to us.

Love is the test of true discipleship. "By this all men will know that you are my disciples, if you love one another" (John 13:35). "My command is this: Love each other as I have loved you" (John 15:12). The true disciple loves. The unloving lay false claim to discipleship.

Love means keeping the commandments. "If you love me, you will obey what I command" (John 14:15). "Whoever has my commands and obeys them, he is the one who loves me" (John 14:21). "If anyone loves me, he will obey my teaching" (John 14:23). "This is love for God: to obey his commands" (1 John 5:3). The Bible does not permit us to confuse true love with warm feelings. Emotional love roams around inside us. What God calls love overflows into deeds done for others, according to the commandments of God. The confusion of feeling with love is not a minor mistake. It appears also in substituting sharing faith for sharing goods. We are quite willing to share our faith with others—something that costs us nothing. Thus, what love requires is sharing goods that cost us a great deal of effort to obtain.

The presence of saving faith is confirmed by love. "For in Christ Jesus neither circumcision nor uncircumcision has any value. The only thing that counts is faith expressing itself through love" (Gal. 5:6). "If I have a faith that can move mountains, but have not love, I am nothing" (1 Cor. 13:2). "As the body without the spirit is dead, so faith without deeds is dead" (James 2:26). "God is love. Whoever lives in love lives in God, and God in him" (1 John 4:16). "Everyone who loves has been born of God and knows God," while "Whoever does not love does not know God, because God is love" (1 John 4:7–8). True believers are obliged to "spur one another on toward love and good deeds" (Heb. 10:24). A saving faith is manifest in a passionate love, and such a love is manifest in good works.

The teaching of the Scriptures is very plain: First, to love is to give: "For God so loved the world that he gave his one and only Son" (John 3:16). For such evidence of love, God himself generously provides us with the gifts we are to share. He first provides what love obliges us to give. Second, love is not optional. That is, giving and sharing are mandatory. Third, giving thus becomes the indelible test of true discipleship. Fourth, love is not warm feelings or fired-up emotions. Love is obedience to the commandment to share. Finally, the believer's claim to saving faith is confirmed by love that generously gives of all that the believer has to share.

WHY GIVE MONEY   5
AND GOODS?

Why should my giving take the form of material things? Would it not be more Christian to share spiritual things? To give away my faith rather than my money? Is it not more obedient to support faith ministries than to give money to the poor who may not merit help or are likely to squander it away? These are serious questions, even if it may be suspected that they are in a preference for sharing faith, which cost us nothing, over sharing goods that we think were hard earned.

The Christian who prepares to answer these queries does well to recall the Lord's healing of ten lepers on the border of Samaria and Galilee. All ten had "stood at a distance and called out in a loud voice, 'Jesus, Master, have pity on us,'" and the Lord did. He healed them all. Then what happened? Only one turned back and gave thanks for his healing, and that one was a Samaritan. In Luke 17:11–19: "Jesus asked, 'Were not all ten cleansed? Where are the other nine? Was no one found to return and give praise to God except this foreigner?'"

Was the Lord unaware *before* the miracle that only one of the lepers would be grateful? Not at all. It is written of him that, "he did not need man's testimony about man, for he knew what was in a man" (John 2:25). Jesus gave healing to all ten lepers, knowing full well that only one would be grateful. Lacking the endless resources of God, we must be prudent in giving, but we must never forget that the Bible knows nothing about "the deserving poor" when it requires sharing goods with them. Rather, all who would be "sons of your Father in heaven" are admonished to follow his example: "He causes his sun to rise on the evil and the good, and sends rain on the righteous and the unrighteous" (Matt. 5:45). The Christian gives money and goods because he is so required by the Scriptures, as the texts quoted throughout this book abundantly demonstrate. For just such material obedience, the Lord gives us the goods that he expects us to share.

There is no biblical license for substituting sharing faith for sharing money and material possessions. This was the burden of Isaiah: "Is not this the kind of fasting I have chosen: to loose the chains of injustice and untie the cords of the yoke, to set the oppressed free and break every yoke? Is it not to share your food with the hungry and to provide the poor wanderer with shelter—when you see the naked, to clothe him, and not to turn away from your own flesh and blood?" (Isa. 58:6–7). Our Lord says: "Give to the one who asks you, and do not turn away from the one who wants to borrow from you" (Matt. 5:42).

The scene of the last judgment so vividly sketched by Christ in Matthew 25:31–46 makes it unmistakable that the evidence of love must be material gifts to the poor: food, drink, warmth, clothing, and the touch of tender care. True love gives in terms of need. Where the need is material, the gift must be material. Where the need is justice, the gift must be the battle to achieve that. Where the need is time, comfort, the use of talent, or skill, the gift must fit it. God gives faith. He who receives faith will give generously of the goods and talents that God has given him.

Has the church no word from the Lord as to exactly how much the believer owes God by way of the church? The answer is yes it has. The believer, because he is a true believer, knows very well that he owes God everything: "For the world is mine, and all that is in it" (Ps. 50:12). God has first claim by right of ownership to everything each of us calls his own. To ask with the psalmist, "How can I repay the LORD for all his goodness to me?" (116:12) can only be completely answered by the acknowledgment: "All, Lord, is thine!"

Moreover, God gives so that his obedient children may give: "And God is able to make all grace abound to you, so that in all things at all times, having all that you need, you will abound in every good work" (2 Cor. 9:8). Can we come no closer than this to some measure of how much we owe the Lord? The Bible teaches that the most ancient measure of what the believer owes to God is the tithe, one-tenth of what God gives to us. The Israelites were obliged to give the Levites one-tenth of the produce of their soil, of their orchards, of their flocks. Additionally, every third year a tithe—probably a second tithe—was to be shared with the stranger and the poor (Lev. 27:30–33; Deut. 12:5–18).

Going further, the Lord required offerings of two basic types: (1) sin offerings and (2) thank offerings. The prophet Malachi charges Israel with robbing God by neglecting both tithes and offerings: "Will a man rob God? Yet you rob me. But you ask, 'How do we rob you?'" "In tithes and offerings. You are under a curse—the whole nation of you—because you are robbing me. Bring the whole tithe into the storehouse, that there may be food in my house. Test me in this," says the LORD Almighty, "and see if I will not throw open the floodgates of heaven and pour out so much blessing that you will not have room enough for it" (Mal. 3:8–10).

There is no suggestion in the Scriptures that the Lord's demand on the Old Testament Israelites is abated for the New Testament church. Nor is there any suggestion that what we give elsewhere can be credited against the tithe owed the church. Indeed, Paul sets a higher standard especially for those who are richly blessed: "On the first day of every week, each one of you should set aside a sum of money in keeping with his income, saving it up, so that when I come no collections will have to be made" (1 Cor. 16:2). The more generous God is, the more generous we should be. Is God pleased, then, with our liberality? Indeed: "For God loves a cheerful giver" (2 Cor. 9:7).

There is, however, one more thing to be added on the matter of how much do we owe the Lord and his church? It is taught us by the familiar story recounted in both Mark and Luke:

> Jesus sat down opposite the place where the offerings were put and watched the crowd putting their money into the temple treasury. Many rich people threw in large amounts. But a poor widow came and put in two very small copper coins, worth only a fraction of a penny.
>
> Calling his disciples to him, Jesus said, "I tell you the truth, this poor widow has put more into the treasury than all the others. They all gave out of their wealth; but she, out of her poverty, put in everything—all she had to live on." (Mark 12:41–44; see also Luke 21:1–4)

By making a point of calling his disciples to him, the Lord intends that we should take careful note of what he has to say. What does he have to say? It is this: God measures the amount of what we give by comparison with the amount we keep for ourselves. The widow gave the most because she kept back nothing. The others gave less because they kept back more. This is not pleasant truth to hear, especially for those who think themselves very generous because their gifts are substantial, and who expect that the church and the Lord will think the same. There must be no mistake about this: The Lord does love the cheerful giver. The Lord does expect those whom he has richly blessed to be richly generous. The Lord accepts each gift as an investment in heaven. Let those who are generous always be appreciated.

When we are asking "how much" do I owe the Lord's work in the church and for the neighbor, then we come finally to the Lord's own measure of how much it is that we should give, say in comparison with one another. His teaching is clear: He who gives the most in the sight of heaven is the one who keeps back the least by comparison. He who gives the least in the sight of heaven is the one who keeps back the most by comparison. This follows from the fact that all we have is God's to begin with. What we give, he gave us to share; what we keep is still his.

The King James Version speaks of the poor widow's gift as "two mites," the smallest Hebrew coins. Mites and millions may loom differently in the sight of God than in ours. Remember, too, that the Bible takes very seriously a dividing line we tend to ignore—the dividing line of death. In terms of giving, death marks the watershed of reward. Generosity that is publicly acknowledged this side of the grave already has its reward. Generosity done without fanfare this side of the grave is rewarded in heaven: "So when you give to the needy, do not announce it with trumpets, as the hypocrites do in the synagogues and on the streets, to be honored by men. I tell you the truth, they have received their reward in full. But when you give to the needy, do not let your left hand know what your right hand is doing, so that your giving may be in secret. Then your Father, who sees what is done in secret, will reward you" (Matt. 6:2–4). When God comes in judgment, on the last day, he will reward: "See, the Sovereign LORD comes with power, and his arm rules for him. See, his reward is with him, and his recompense accompanies him" (Isa. 40:10). For this reason the apostle can say, "Let us not become weary in doing good, for at the proper time we will reap a harvest if we do not give up" (Gal. 6:9).

In times of discouragement, take heart from the knowledge that both quietly and all about us service is seen taking place and is known by God to be rewarded later: "I tell you the truth, anyone who gives you a cup of water in my name because you belong to Christ will certainly not lose his reward" (Mark 9:41). Reward-bearing service is out of the reach of no one, but reward-seeking notoriety risks having all the praise it will receive from men rather than from God. The Lord's warning is unmistakable: "Be careful not to do your 'acts of righteousness' before men, to be seen by them. If you do, you will have no reward from your Father in heaven" (Matt. 6:1).

One thing more: Tithing as a measure of good stewardship does not only apply to money and goods. It applies no less to time, talent, skills, and personal services of all kinds. Where money or goods will meet a need, then money or goods the steward must, if he can, provide. The common criticism of the welfare system that it tries to solve all problems by "throwing money at them" applies no less to good stewarding. There are things that money cannot buy, such as genuine friendship, persistent compassion, the thoughtful word or call, the affirming glance or warming smile. These, too, fall under the claim of the Lord upon a tithe of our capacities. Happily, these are within the reach of everyone who remembers to share them. Life itself, in all of the forms it can take, is ours to steward—for years three-score and ten, if the Lord wills. Consider every good that you can do for another a part of the tithe claimed by the Lord. Remember that he speaks not only of tithes but also, and in addition, of that second mile, the offerings.

SACRIFICE AND STEWARDSHIP

Christians are described in Scripture as "a royal priesthood" (1 Peter 2:9). The apostle picks up here God's description of his people Israel: "You will be for me a kingdom of priests and a holy nation" (Ex. 19:6). What does it mean that true believers are priests and belong to a royal priesthood? It means that the Christian, as king, so rules over himself that, as priest, he sacrifices his own self-interests to those of others. This is a royal priesthood.

SACRIFICE: WHAT IT IS AND WHAT IT MEANS

Sacrifice is at the very heart of Christianity. The vicarious self-sacrifice of Jesus Christ on Calvary highlights the fact that sacrifice is of the essence of our religion. The believer does not avoid sacrifice through faith in Jesus. It is a true and living faith that makes the believer's priestly self-sacrifice possible. True Christians are, as the Bible declares, "a royal priesthood." That is to say, true Christians are good stewards.

For example, a little child disobeys his mother, and then he goes out and picks a wild flower for her. Why? Partly because he hopes that by doing so, he will appease her annoyance and lighten his probable punishment. More fundamentally, however, he wants to get "right" with his mother again by making an "offering" that will erase the wrong that separates them and that troubles his conscience. Sacrifice is like that. It is an offering given to a higher authority to undo the effects of disobedience and to make things right again.

Sacrifice reaches far back into the history of Christianity as well as into other forms of religion. We deal here only with sacrifice in Christianity where it is fundamental. We know that God created man good and in his own image (Gen. 1:26–27) and that man breaks the divine law and thus alienates himself and his descendents from his Creator (Gen. 3:1–20). Estranged from God, man early turns to sacrifice. Cain and Abel, the first two sons of Adam and Eve, bring their offerings to God (Gen. 4:3–4). Noah sacrifices to God after the flood (Gen. 8:20). Abraham (whose name was at first Abram) builds an altar to commemorate God's promise to him of the land of Canaan for his descendents (Gen. 15:17–18).

When the Lord liberates Israel from slavery in Egypt, he lays down rules that make sacrifice the heart of worship. He requires the Levites, descendents of Jacob's third son Levi, to be servants of the altar and later in the temple. The tribe of Levi inherits no land in Canaan. So unique is their service to God and his people that they live off the gifts that are presented by other tribes to the Lord: "Therefore Levi has no portion or inheritance with his brothers; the Lord is his inheritance, as the Lord your God said to him" (Deut. 10:9).

The Levites provide a dual service. First, Aaron, brother to Moses, and all his descendents are priests. They serve at the altar, making sacrifices with the peoples' gifts to the Lord. Second, all other descendents of Levi are called Levites, and their service is to prepare the peoples' gifts for sacrifice and to care for all the tasks involving the temple. We commonly read, therefore, of "the priests and Levites" as occupying offices in the temple.

For a detailed outline of Israel's sacrificial system, consult a Bible dictionary. What concerns us here is that the temple sacrifices were of two basic kinds: (1) offerings made for sins, and (2) offerings made in thanksgiving—both for forgiveness of sins and for God's many other blessings.

What, however, was the meaning of the sacrificial system imposed by God upon Israel? The priests offered the peoples' sacrifices on the temple altar. In so doing, they foreshadowed Christ's sacrifice of himself. As the New Testament epistle to the Hebrews makes clear, the temple sacrifices come to their culmination in the death of Jesus on the cross. With this act, the work of the priests and Levites came to fulfillment. The altar of the Old Testament church then becomes the table of the Lord's Supper in the New Testament church.

The sacrificial system thus found its meaning, and the symbol of the altar has given way to the symbol of the table—though in essence both imply the same thing: sacrifice. Old Testament sacrifices consisted of animals, birds, and the firstfruits of the harvest. These were things that the giver might have used for himself. Thus, sacrifice was self-sacrifice too. The giver surrenders to the Lord and to the temple what he could have made use of. This is the first step in sacrifice: Give to God what you could use for yourself.

This, however, was only the first step because God sees the heart of the giver. Does the sin offering reflect a heart truly repentant and truly determined to amend its ways? This is what genuine sacrifice for sin required—an outward symbol of an inward state. If the heart was and is not true, the sacrifice is not acceptable to God. He makes this clear, again and again, through his prophets: "Does the LORD delight in burnt offerings and sacrifices as much as in obeying the voice of the LORD? To obey is better than sacrifice, and to heed is better than the fat of rams" (1 Sam. 15:22). This is the Word of the Lord spoken by Samuel the Lord's prophet, to Saul, first king of Israel.

To those whose heart was not in accord with their offerings, the Lord declared: "Stop bringing meaningless offerings. Your incense is detestable to me. When you spread out your hands in prayer, I will hide my eyes from you; even if you offer many prayers, I will not listen. Your hands are full of blood" (Isa. 1:13, 15). How then does sacrifice become acceptable? The Lords answers: "Wash and make yourselves clean. Take your evil deeds out of my sight. Stop doing wrong, learn to do right. Seek justice, encourage the oppressed. Defend the cause of the fatherless, plead the case of the widow" (Isa. 1:15–17). "Is not this the kind of fasting I have chosen: to loose the chains of injustice and untie the cords of the yoke, to set the oppressed free and break every yoke? Is it not to share your food with the hungry and to provide the poor wanderer with shelter—when you see the naked, to clothe him, and not to turn away from your own flesh and blood?" (Isa. 58:6–7).

The temple sacrifices must represent willing *self*-sacrifice for others, or the temple sacrifices are unacceptable. The believer must love God above all (Deut. 6:5) and show it by loving neighbor as self (Lev. 19:18). This is the meaning of the sacrificial system. Where, however, will the believer find the strength to deny self-interest and practice self-sacrifice? How can the believer obey the command, "Wash and make yourselves clean"? Is not this just what sacrifice was supposed to do? How then can one come to sacrifice with already clean hands? Old Testament sacrifice was of two kinds: (1) for sin and (2) in thanksgiving. The first provided clean hands for the second. The sacrifice of thanksgiving could not reach God unless it rose out of a heart cleansed of sin and thus liberated to obedience. The second, the sacrifice of thanksgiving was acceptable to God only if it reflected the will to a life of obedience as required by God. This is the burden of the prophets, as we have observed. This was not the life of perfection, for then the sacrifice for sin would no longer be necessary. It was the life striving for perfection, through obedience to divine law. The temple sacrifices for sin only symbolized the true sacrifice for sin—Christ's self-sacrifice on the altar of Calvary. When that happened, the table of the Lord took the place of the altar, and the Old Testament Levitical office had run its course. The ministry to the altar ended and reappeared in a new ministry to another table.

Now the congregation gathers around the Lord's Table as he commanded (Matt. 26:26–28; 1 Cor. 11:23–26). There the believer is once again confirmed in his liberation from sin and selfishness. He is once more stimulated to self-sacrifice through the gift of goods, time, and talent to the Lord. However, the thankful church must deliver its gifts to the Lord another way. The service required by God of Israel was symbolized in the temple sacrifice, representing self-sacrifice for the neighbor. Ministering to this sacrifice were the Levites. The service required by God of the New Israel, the New Testament church, is in the temples where God now chooses to be found and worshipped—the Christian. Thus, the writer to Hebrews first explains the transition from the Old Testament service to the New Testament gospel and then relates this to the believer's response: "Do not forget to do good and to share with others, for with such sacrifices God is pleased" (Heb. 13:16).

It now becomes clear why all believers are described in Scripture as being themselves priests. God says to Israel: "You will be for me a kingdom of priests and a holy nation" (Ex. 19:6). Peter writes: "Come to him, the living Stone—rejected by men but chosen by God and precious to him—you also, like living stones, are being built into a spiritual house to be a holy priesthood, offering spiritual sacrifices acceptable to God through Jesus Christ" (1 Peter 2:4–5). John writes in Revelation: "To him who loves us and has freed us from our sins by his blood, and has made us to be a kingdom and priests to serve his God and Father—to him be glory and power for ever and ever! Amen" (Rev. 1:5–6).

A priest presides at sacrifice. The believer as priest presides at the daily sacrifice of his own selfishness and gives the fruits of such self-sacrifice to God: "Therefore, I urge you, brothers, in view of God's mercy, to offer your bodies as living sacrifices, holy and pleasing to God—this is your spiritual act of worship" (Rom. 12:1). Such sacrifice can range from the smallest act of self-denial done in obedience through the sharing of goods, talents, time, energies with others, to the very sacrifice of life itself: "Greater love has no one than this, that he lay down his life for his friends" (John 15:13).

Thus, the divine plan comes full circle—from the foreshadowing of Calvary in the Old Testament priesthood and Levites through the liberating reality of Christ's own fulfillment of the promise to the believer's thankful response in the priestly sacrifice of himself for the good of others—in short, Christians, be good stewards.

LEVELS OF AWARENESS: 8
FAITH AND WORKS

As a believer you will understand at some level the relationship between faith and good works as it applies to your exercise of Christian stewardship. There are four levels.

LEVEL ONE: SALVATION

At this stage, all emphasis falls on salvation by faith. There is no relationship between salvation and service.

The Bible declares: "For it is by grace you have been saved, through faith—and this not from yourselves, it is the gift of God—not by works, so that no one can boast" (Eph. 2:8–9). Assurance of salvation exists, at this stage, by itself. If the believer thinks at all in terms of charity to the needy, it is as something added to salvation. The believer's focus is far more on sharing the faith than on sustaining a ministry of service to the poor. Congregational offerings are taken for evangelism. Acts of charity are thought largely to be the responsibility of the individual believer as the Spirit moves him. Theologically, grace is stressed as opposed to the law's being stressed or the New Testament in contrast to the Old. Any talk of good works is likely to be interpreted as the social gospel, or as a futile effort to gain heaven by one's own exertions. Additionally, self-sacrificial stewardship may seem largely optional.

LEVEL TWO: VOLUNTARY GRATITUDE

The believer is indeed saved by grace. This is a fundamental truth that the Bible repeats over and over: "For all have sinned and fall short of the glory of God, and are justified freely by his grace through the redemption that came by Christ Jesus" (Rom. 3:23–24). "As far as the east is from the west, so far has he removed our transgressions from us" (Ps. 103:12).

Thinking on such unmerited salvation, believers find themselves moved to gratitude. Moreover, they are aware that gratitude must be more than lip service. Does not the prophet Isaiah condemn "These people come near to me with their mouth and honor me with their lips, but their hearts are far from me" (Isa. 29:13)? This is a judgment reinforced by the Lord himself (Matt. 15:8–9). Much of the congregation's effort to give material expression to their gratitude may still go into the support of evangelism, both that of the congregation itself and that of radio and television crusaders. However, gratitude may also take the form of charity. It is here that stewardship has moved from the optional to the desirable.

LEVEL THREE: MANDATORY GRATITUDE

Reading on in Paul's letter to the Ephesians, just past the point quoted under Level One above, the believer is told: "For we are God's workmanship, created in Christ Jesus to do good works, which God prepared in advance for us to do" (Eph. 2:10).

We are not saved *by doing* good works, but we are saved *for doing* them. Reflecting on the significance of this and similar biblical teaching, the congregation move into two new levels of awareness.

The first is that salvation is both individual and communal. Faith unites believers both to Jesus Christ and to his body, the church. Each is a *member*, that is, a living part of the whole congregation. Paul graphically describes what such membership in the church means in 1 Corinthians 12. Paul says, for example, that God distributes various gifts to members of the church so that, by mutual service and dependence, the body is drawn the closer together: "That its parts should have equal concern for each other. If one part suffers, every part suffers with it; if one part is honored, every part rejoices with it" (1 Cor. 12:25–26); "There are different kinds of gifts, but the same Spirit. There are different kinds of service, but the same Lord. There are different kinds of working, but the same God works all of them in all men" (1 Cor. 12:4–6).

The second is when congregations become aware that in that

the members of the body present a powerful witness to the world: "Live such good lives among the pagans that, though they accuse you of doing wrong, they may see your good deeds and glorify God on the day he visits us" (1 Peter 2:12). The congregation finds itself with being concerned for each other, and they should rejoice in the reminder to: "Let your light shine before men, that they may see your good deeds and praise your Father in heaven" (Matt. 5:16). At this stage stewardship is recognized as necessary.

LEVEL FOUR: FAITH IS GOOD WORKS

The Lord asks: "Who are my mother and my brothers?" Then he answers: "Whoever does God's will is my brother and sister and mother" (Mark 3:33, 35). At this level in Christian awareness it is perceived that faith and behavior merge. We are no longer able to separate salvation by faith from the doing of good works through faith in obedience to the will (that is, law) of God. The desire to do good, in gratitude for salvation, is now seen not simply as evidence of rebirth in Christ Jesus, it *is* rebirth in Christ Jesus. Doing good is the other face of being saved—for it is to doing good that we are saved. Or, better, we enter into salvation through obedience that is displayed in good works. This is evident throughout the Scriptures.

To believe in Jesus as Savior is to obey Christ as Lord: "We know that we have come to know him if we obey his commands" (1 John 2:3); "If you love me, you will obey what I command" (John 14:15); "Not everyone who says to me, 'Lord, Lord,' will enter the kingdom of heaven, but only he who does the will of my Father who is in heaven" (Matt. 7:21). Those who believe obey, and those who obey believe:

> Therefore everyone who hears these words of mine and puts them into practice is like a wise man who built his house on the rock. The rain came down, the streams rose, and the winds blew and beat against that house; yet it did not fall, because it had its foundation on the rock. (Matt. 7:24–25)

> Do not merely listen to the word, and so deceive yourselves. Do what it says. But the man who looks intently into the perfect law that gives freedom, and continues to do this,

not forgetting what he has heard, but doing it—he will be blessed in what he does. (James 1:22, 25)

To know God is to do justice, as is seen in the following passages.

"Did not your father have food and drink? He did what was right and just, so all went well with him. He defended the cause of the poor and needy, and so all went well. Is that not what it means to know me?" declares the LORD. (Jer. 22:15–16)

Is not this the kind of fasting I have chosen: to loose the chains of injustice and untie the cords of the yoke, to set the oppressed free and break every yoke? Is it not to share your food with the hungry and to provide the poor wanderer with shelter—when you see the naked, to clothe him, and not to turn away from your own flesh and blood? Then your light will break forth like the dawn. (Isa. 58:6–8)

The prophet Isaiah declares: "They will neither harm nor destroy on all my holy mountain, for the earth will be full of the knowledge of the LORD as the waters cover the sea" (Isa. 11:9). The knowledge of God is the doing of right, that is, the doing of his will.

The believer is required to love: "Let no debt remain outstanding, except the continuing debt to love one another, for he who loves his fellowman has fulfilled the law" (Rom. 13:8); "The entire law is summed up in a single command: 'Love your neighbor as yourself'" (Gal. 5:14). And the Lord adds this: "By this all men will know that you are my disciples, if you love one another" (John 13:35).

At this level of awareness, stewardship registers its activity by the spiritual temperature of the believer. Good works witness the love for the body and for the world much as a thermometer registers warmth of weather.

Here priestly self-sacrifice is recognized as being indispensable.

Attaining Level Four

Obviously, level-four awareness is *the* believer's goal. Can this level be found? If so, how will you go about that? Begin with the knowledge that the life of love is not natural to us. By nature, we are ruled by self-interest, but the Lord requires a life of self-sacrifice. The gradual substitution from the will of self-interest to the will of self-sacrifice is what progress in the Christian life consists of. The goal of the church itself is to promote the life of love in each member of the congregation. How does the church, then, go about seeking level-four awareness? Begin by preaching the Word: "Consequently, faith comes from hearing the message, and the message is heard through the word of Christ" (Rom. 10:17). Faith matures more and more into the life of love under persistent preaching of the Scriptures: "All Scripture is God-breathed and is useful for teaching, rebuking, correcting and training in righteousness, so that the man of God may be thoroughly equipped for every good work" (2 Tim. 3:16–17). Preaching is always the key, and the congregation set on a hill by the witness of its good works is evidently the place where the Word of God is most effectively preached.

Those who ardently desire to develop the gift of faith can diligently seek to do the works of faith. The Bible clearly specifies which works a true faith leads the believer to do: "The fruit of the Spirit is love, joy, peace, patience, kindness, goodness, faithfulness, gentleness and self-control" (Gal. 5:22–23). "Love is patient, love is kind. It does not envy, it does not boast, it is not proud. It is not rude, it is not self-seeking, it is not easily angered, it keeps no record of wrongs. Love does not delight in evil but rejoices with the truth. It always protects, always trusts, always hopes, always perseveres" (1 Cor. 13:4–7). An effort to live such a life of love opens the heart to greater possession by faith.

Again and again, the Old Testament prophets, as well as Christ himself, stress the fact that a hard heart presents a deaf ear to the Word; the heart is hardened by persistent refusal to support the needy and to do good works among men. All who seek to open their hearts to the Spirit and the Word can prepare the soil in which faith finds fruit by doing the works of faith through presenting themselves where the Word is truly preached.

In summary, Christian stewardship is not an accidental, optional, or perhaps haphazard series of handouts given by Christians and the church on their way to glory. Good, personal stewardship is the way to glory, and the more certainly the congregation is on its way to heaven the more certainly will its *works* testify to the love of God.

INVESTMENT AND RETURN

God and Free Enterprise

The Lord God is a free enterpriser. This is one reason why Karl Marx, who was not a free enterpriser, rejected God.

God is a free enterpriser because he expects a return on his investments. Jesus' parables of the talents (Matt. 25:14–30) and of the ten minas (Luke 19:11–27) clearly teach us that God expects interest on the talents he invests in each of us. This is implied in the Lord's command: "Be perfect, therefore, as your heavenly Father is perfect" (Matt. 5:48).

In short, all of God's gifts to mankind are as a divine investment on which the investor expects full return. We know from the whole tenor of the Scriptures what the nature of that return should be: so putting our talents at God's disposal that others derive benefit from the gifts given to us. This is summarized in the Golden Rule: "Do to others as you would have them do to you" (Luke 6:31).

This ideal order of return on divine investment is shattered by sin. Paul vividly describes it: "They exchanged the truth of God for a lie, and worshiped and served created things rather than the Creator—who is forever praised" (Rom. 1:25). Paul goes on to detail the consequences of this substitution of the lie for the truth:

> They have become filled with every kind of wickedness, evil, greed and depravity. They are full of envy, murder,

strife, deceit and malice. They are gossips, slanderers, God-
haters, insolent, arrogant and boastful; they invent ways of
doing evil; they disobey their parents; they are senseless,
faithless, heartless, ruthless. Although they know God's
righteous decree that those who do such things deserve
death, they not only continue to do these very things but
also approve of those who practice them." (Rom. 1:29–32)

The divine investor is willfully defrauded of his return. At the
heart of this theft is false worship. Men bow before their own lusts
instead of before their Creator, because they are in bondage to the
Devil, author of the lie.

Out of Egypt

Israel's bondage in Egypt symbolizes mankind's bondage to sin
and Satan. The Lord's liberation of Israel from Egyptian bondage symbolizes his liberation of all true believers from bondage to
self-interest and Satan, through the self-sacrificial death of Jesus
Christ. On Jesus the Lord laid "the iniquity of us all" (Isa. 53:6),
so that by faith the believer is "free from the law of sin and death"
(Rom. 8:2).

What, then, is this "by faith" that frees us from Egyptian
bondage? It is the gift of God that sets us once more in the position of returning God some interest on his investment in us. Our
gifts and talents are liberated from bondage to self-lust and freed
for service to others in the name of God. To all those liberated by
faith are the parables of the talents and of the ten minas addressed.

Then What?

Believers are not left in the dark as to how the Lord wants interest
upon his investment of talents and gifts. The Word of God sheds
light upon the ways in which interest accrues. God himself con-
nects our liberation with obedience to his commandments: "I am
the LORD your God, who brought you out of Egypt, out of the
land of slavery. "You shall have no other gods before me" (Ex.
20:2–3). Liberation is under the Law, not from the Law: "Do not
think that I have come to abolish the Law or the Prophets; I have
not come to abolish them but to fulfill them. I tell you the truth,
until heaven and earth disappear, not the smallest letter, not the

least stroke of a pen, will by any means disappear from the Law until everything is accomplished" (Matt. 5:17–18).

The commandments are summarized in the divine requirements to love God above all and our neighbors as ourselves (Luke 10:27). These are the twin guides to producing interest on God's investment in ourselves.

The motif of investment-return appears in the Great Commission of the New Testament. The apostles are mandated by the Christ to build his church. First, they are to preach the good news (gospel) of liberation. Those who believe the good news are joined to the church through baptism. And the church is then obliged to teach them all that the Lord commands, which is how to produce a return upon God's investment in them (Matt. 28:19–20). And what the Lord commands is nothing else than what was summarized by the commandments given Israel after liberation from Egypt, and expounded by the prophets throughout Israel's history—and further applied by the apostolic epistles to the New Testament church.

God's Agents

Like any prudent investor, God does not leave his return to chance. He pursues it, and his agent in this pursuit is his church, where good stewardship is taught and practiced.

CONSCIENCE

Stewardship has a watchful monitor in the conscience. Consider carefully, therefore, what the conscience does.

We do not say, "what the conscience *is*." Fruitless hours of speculation can be spent on what conscience *is*. It can be questioned whether or not all persons have a conscience, and if so whether it is acquired by birth or developed by environment. Avoid such detours by focusing upon how conscience behaves, what it does, and why that can be enlisted in service.

What Conscience Does

The term *conscience* implies "knowing together," or "knowing with," at one and the same time: from *con* meaning "with" and *science* meaning "knowledge."

What, then, is known together by conscience? Two things: (1) the divine law, spelled out in the Ten Commandments and inscribed by God upon the human heart as part of the divine image in each human being; and, (2) the action one has done, or contemplates doing; the thoughts and purposes one entertains; in short, all behavior. Conscience brings law and conduct together, and judges behavior by the Law. Conscience is the inner courtroom where God's Word and our conduct meet for judgment. Conscience is God's witness in each human heart: "They show that the requirements of the law are written on their hearts, their consciences also bearing witness" (Rom. 2:15). Paul is here speaking of those to whom the Law did not come by special revelation, the Gentiles.

Conscience monitors behavior, makes demands upon it in the name of the Law. And in response, the believer can strive to keep his conscience clear of accusation against him by seeking to obey God's Law—and here conscience becomes ally to the believer and to the church. Paul says to the Roman governor Felix: "So I strive always to keep my conscience clear before God and man" (Acts 24:16). That is to say, the Christian always strives to love, which is obedience to the Law.

Bridge to the Particular

Conscience plays a unique role in the obedient life.

It is often said that the Bible falls short of particulars in laying down regulations for Christian obedience. We are never expressly told, for example, how much we may keep for ourselves of all the goods that God gives us. We are not informed as to whether money should be given to one charity or to another, or whether it is right to enjoy good food and drink while many starve. The Bible declines to be an ethical recipe book. The Word only reveals general mandates and universal commandments.

Why? Because God provides conscience to be the bridge from the general and universal law to the particular act. Conscience is, so to speak, the elbow where the vertical command coming down from God governs the horizontal deed done among men.

The Bible is geared to conscience. The Word is addressed to conscience, and should be preached to conscience. Out of the struggle to do the revealed will of God in daily living, conscience emerges ever more sensitive and helpful. Conscience is the agent of Christian maturity.

Always Reliable?

It is easy to dispute the trustworthiness of conscience. "Let your conscience be your guide" is indeed not always a guarantee that what follows is in full accord with divine Law. The conscience requires a constant tutor—the Word of God. Believers bring conscience to the worship service to school it the better in awakening response to the Law—the version written on the conscience vibrating in harmony with the preaching of what is written in the Scriptures.

Estranged from the church, and indifferent to the Bible, conscience may indeed become more and more wayward and less and less reliable: "Furthermore, since they did not think it worthwhile to retain the knowledge of God, he gave them over to a depraved mind, to do what ought not to be done" (Rom. 1:28).

But aroused again and again by the Word preached, tutored by the Word studied, and disciplined by an alert eldership, the believer's conscience serves as the living voice of the Word, "now accusing, now even defending" what he thinks, says, and does (Rom. 2:15).

Conscience is there. We need not, and could not, create it. But how exciting a challenge to enlist its voice in our efforts to serve the Christ through obedience to the divine Law in the form of good stewardship.

"The LORD sends poverty and wealth" (1 Sam. 2:7).

Could not God immediately feed all the world's hungry? Indeed, he could. This is evident from the miracles done by Jesus with the loaves and fishes (Matt. 14:17–21). He reminds his disciples: "Don't you remember the five loaves for the five thousand, and how many basketfuls you gathered? Or the seven loaves of the four thousand and how many baskets you gathered?" (Matt. 16:9–10). Twice the Lord multiplied a lad's lunch into a meal fed to thousands of men and women, with plenty left over.

God fed Israel with manna, rained from the sky in the wilderness, and even varied the diet with the meat of quail (Ex. 16). He instructed ravens to feed the prophet Elijah with bread and meat, morning and evening; and provided that the supply of meal and oil should not fail in the home of the widow of Zarephath "every day" (1 Kings 17:6, 8–16).

There is more than enough evidence in Scripture to assure us that God could, at will, satisfy human need around the globe.

But he does not. Why not?

Because the needy serve God's purpose, and have their own recompense for so doing.

God's Purpose

How shall those who truly love the Lord manifest their love for him in deeds? How shall believers give their Savior material expression of their love when, in fact, all is already his and he, being perfect, needs nothing?

God provides the needy to solve this problem. He wills to be sought, found, and served in the poor. This is clear from what has already been said about investment in heaven. It is clear, too, from the parable of the last judgment, where the Lord equates gifts made to the poor as made to him: "I tell you the truth, whatever you did for one of the least of these brothers of mine, you did for me" (Matt. 25:40).

The poor and needy are God's surrogates. We serve him through them. That is why there are poor in God's world. And to compensate for the burden of poverty, as we shall see, God gives the needy special blessing.

Secular Explanations

The secular mind attempts many explanations for poverty. Behind them all, the Bible gives us but one fundamental account: "The LORD sends poverty and wealth."

The difference between the secular explanations and the Bible's account is of crucial importance to believers, in discerning that the poor are not so much a problem as an answer. God provides the needy so that the Christian can answer the question: Why give? Why give in money and material goods?

Secular explanations account for poverty from some inferred causes, such as: The poor are lazy, the poor are shiftless, the poor cannot handle money, they do not know how to save, they cannot restrain their desires, they lack employable skills, they cannot hold jobs, they will not take orders, they are victimized by their own subculture, and so forth. All of which may be, indeed, God's means to poverty.

As secondary causes, they do provide Christians with the challenge to set right what can be amended. There will always be poor enough in the world so that the Lord can bless every serious effort to prevent poverty. But the underlying meaning of poverty is the Lord's will to provide opportunity to the true believer to display love in deed. This becomes evident in the fact that countless millions of poor humans slave at jobs from dawn to dusk and remain poverty- stricken just the same. God makes poor . . . .

Jesus tells a parable (Matt. 20:1–16) that enforces what is revealed through Samuel. A landowner, Jesus says, goes out early in the morning to hire men to work in his vineyard. Some he finds and hires early in the morning, some later in the day, and still others well toward evening. When evening came, the owner of the vineyard instructs his foreman to pay each worker the very same wage. Some who had labored through the heat of day complain that those who had worked but a little get the same reward. To which the landowner (God) responds: "Don't I have the right to do what I want with my own money?" (Matt. 20:15). God, the Creator and owner of all things, does his will with the world's goods. He makes poor and rich, by giving and withholding what is his own.

We note, in passing, that poverty is the thing of which revolution is made. Marxism rests its appeal on the misery of the proletariat. The Bible, too, has a response to that misery: obedience among the rich and powerful to the commandments of God.

Moses takes account of this option in addressing the church as it appeared in the form of Israel: "However, there should be no poor among you, for in the land the LORD your God is giving you to possess as your inheritance, he will richly bless you, if only you fully obey the LORD your God and are careful to follow all these commands I am giving you today" (Deut. 15:4–5). This, then, becomes the New Testament church's ideal: There need be no poverty around the world, if only God's commandment to love were universally obeyed. Such should be the goal of missions and evangelism.

God does, indeed, make poor so the Scriptures teach, but he does so, as it were, against his will. God's command to love him above all is fulfilled in that love for neighbor that makes the elimination of poverty its prime goal.

Jesus is, alas, so certain that the commandment of God will not be universally obeyed, that he can say: "You will always have the poor among you, but you will not always have me" (John 12:8). Marxism will not, either, scourge poverty from the face of the globe. As Moses himself had acknowledged: "There will always be poor people in the land" (Deut. 15:11)—that is, on account of our disobedience.

Divine Compensation

God goes out of his way, however, throughout the Bible, to reveal an intense concern for the poor whom he provides as opportunity to the rich, in ways such as the following:

God hears their cries of distress: "The LORD hears the needy" (Ps. 69:33). *Hears* means, in Scripture, "acts upon." God responds to the pleas of the oppressed and needy. Many a head lies restless on its pillow because God has heard the groans of those oppressed by its owner. Many a business failure took first root in deceit against the unwary. God hears when the victims of injustice cry to him.

God supplies spiritual strength to the poor so that they may transcend their lives of grinding hardship: "You have been a refuge for the poor, a refuge for the needy in his distress" (Isa. 25:4). The endurance of the oppressed in the face of apparently insurmountable odds is God-given. The peace that may pervade a poor dwelling descends from above. The sweet sleep of the dead-tired may contrast with the restlessness of the rich. God makes poor and compensates in his own way for their tragedy.

Though poverty commonly affords little hope of temporal escape for those caught in its toils, God promises that "the needy will not always be forgotten, nor the hope of the afflicted ever perish" (Ps. 9:18). The Lord lifts the eyes of the needy beyond the narrow horizons of their time-bound lives and gives them hope that lays hold on another, fairer world.

The promise given the poor is precise and explicit: "Because of the oppression of the weak and the groaning of the needy, I will now arise," says the LORD. "I will protect them from those who malign them." (Ps. 12:5). The veil between time and eternity wears thin in poverty, and God lets the needy look easily beyond the narrow confines of their earthly lives. Consider the triumphant songs of the oppressed.

To accomplish these things among those whom he has made poor, God endows them liberally with faith: "Has not God chosen those who are poor in the eyes of the world to be rich in faith and to inherit the kingdom he promised those who love him?" (James 2:5). This is why the risen Christ can instruct John to write to the Church of Smyrna, "I know your afflictions and your poverty— yet you are rich!" (Rev. 2:9). Poor in goods but rich in faith and sure promises.

It is not surprising, then, that Mary magnifies the joy of Jesus' birth by singing that the Lord "has brought down rulers from their thrones but has lifted up the humble. He has filled the hungry with good things but has sent the rich away empty" (Luke

1:52–53). Jesus is food of hope and promise of liberation to the poor, but those rich who will not share their goods, in Jesus' name, find nothing in the Christ for themselves. Their hands full of unshared possessions, they are sent spiritually empty away by a Lord they will not serve with their hoarded goods. The Christ himself confirms his mother's prediction, saying at his home in Nazareth, "The Spirit of the Lord is on me, because he has anointed me to preach good news to the poor" (Luke 4:18)—words taken from the Prophet, said many years before (Isa. 61:1). God compensates those whom he makes poor in goods with the riches of the good news of Jesus Christ.

Having made the poor vulnerable to the greedy, the Lord keeps jealous watch over their treatment: "The LORD enters into judgment against the elders and leaders of his people: 'It is you who have ruined my vineyard; the plunder from the poor is in your houses. What do you mean by crushing my people and grinding the faces of the poor?'" (Isa. 3:14–15). The wicked prove themselves wicked by taking advantage of those whom the Lord has made temporally defenseless: "In his arrogance the wicked man hunts down the weak, who are caught in the schemes he devises. He lies in wait like a lion in cover; he lies in wait to catch the helpless; he catches the helpless and drags them off in his net" (Ps. 10:2, 9). God takes special note of evil done to those whom he has made poor. For that sin he destroys Sodom, raining down fire from on high (Gen. 19:24–25).

It was Sodom's fatal crime that she neglected the poor and exploited those whom God had rendered weak: "Now this was the sin of your sister Sodom: She and her daughters were arrogant, overfed and unconcerned; they did not help the poor and needy" (Ezek. 16:49).

IN SUMMARY

Why, then, has God made many poor, and expends such concern over them? Believers should reflect, as they review what has been said so far, on the parable of the rich man and Lazarus (Luke 16:19–31).

What was the poor beggar doing at the rich man's gate? All he asked for food was the scraps discarded from the rich man's sumptuous table. He seems to do the rich man no service. He waits in vain for love expressed in charity. Then Lazarus dies, and lo, he appears in heaven.

Why?

Because, no doubt, he had richly served God's purposes by patiently bearing the heavy yoke of poverty. Lazarus accepted without complaint the burdens laid by God on his shoulders. And what service, then, did Lazarus do for God?

He put the rich man to the test.

God made Lazarus materially poor so that the rich man might be spiritually blessed. Opportunity to show love for God in doing good to Lazarus was on the rich man's very doorstep. He could not come or go from his residence without observing the knock of God on his hard heart.

The rich man failed the test. He, too, like Lazarus, died—and went straight to hell.

The Lord could not more graphically portray the role of the poor in God's world. At issue in this drama, which is played everywhere around the world, was not so much Lazarus' need as the rich man's soul at issue everywhere that poverty appears is God's test of man's soul. For the poor it is a question of patient endurance of God's yoke. For the rich it is a question of love working through material goods.

The judgment is sure: "Depart from me, you who are cursed, into the eternal fire prepared for the devil and his angels. For I was hungry and you gave me nothing to eat, I was thirsty and you gave me nothing to drink, I was a stranger and you did not invite me in, I needed clothes and you did not clothe me, I was sick and in prison and you did not look after me" (Matt. 25:41–43).

The mystery of poverty is that God uses the needy to stand in his stead among all the nations of the world. Because their yoke is burdensome, God lightens their plight with excess of faith, hope, and love. And through them God tests: (1) Those whose service to him is in talk only, mere lip service. (2) Those who cannot resist the temptation to take advantage of the weak. (3) Those who, in their eagerness to display their love, seek him out in the needy where he may be found, and give of their goods, time, talents, and skills to them.

THE MYSTERY
OF WEALTH

"The silver is mine and the gold is mine," declares the LORD Almighty. (Hag. 2:8)

No sound perspective on the church's duty toward the wealthy is possible apart from this revealed truth: All wealth, however acquired, is God's, let out on strictly temporary loan to whoever is its temporal possessor. So crucial is this fundamental Christian economic maxim that we repeat it, and urge that the congregation be persistently reminded of the Lord's repeated declaration: "For the world is mine, and all that is in it" (Ps. 50:12). Israel's King David, who himself accumulated vast public and personal sums in preparation for building the Lord's temple in Jerusalem, declares: "Wealth and honor come from you; you are the ruler of all things" (1 Chron. 29:12).

Even the very effort through which anyone acquires temporal title to God's material gifts is itself his donation: "But remember the LORD your God, for it is he who gives you the ability to produce wealth" (Deut. 8:18).

All this, we repeat, is background and context for the church's approach to the mystery of wealth.

IN EXCHANGE

In exchange for his gifts, as we have pointed out, the Lord exacts return. God is, as we have said, a free enterpriser, demanding interest on his loans to mankind in proportion to the gift: "From everyone who has been given much, much will be demanded" (Luke 12:48). But how shall the recipient of wealth know what is "required" of him in exchange for its temporal use? Only those who ask this question seriously receive an answer: "It is written in the Prophets: 'They will all be taught by God'" (John 6:45; Jesus is quoting Isaiah 54:13).

How does God now teach?

By his Word, the Holy Scripture, most authoritatively as that Word is preached *in* the church by those ordained *by* the church to the task: "And how can they hear without someone preaching to them? And how can they preach unless they are sent?" (Rom. 10:14–15).

To use a biblical illustration, the world is the Lord's vineyard, and "Who plants a vineyard and does not eat of its grapes?" (1 Cor. 9:7). In a more restricted sense, we may transpose the language of the prophet to say, using "church" instead of "Israel": "The vineyard of the LORD Almighty is the house of Israel, and the men of Judah are the garden of his delight" (Isa. 5:7).

It is within the church that the question is most seriously asked: How shall we know what the divine owner of the vineyard whose fruits we enjoy "requires" of us? It is within the church that the answer is seriously supplied: "Your word is a lamp to my feet and a light for my path" (Ps. 119:105). It is within the church that the call goes out: "Come, O house of Jacob, let us walk in the light of the LORD" (Isa. 2:5). And it is within the church that the scientific light shed by economics on the uses of wealth is set in the light of the inspired Word: "In your light we see [our] light" (Ps. 36:9).

WHAT DOES THE CHURCH SAY?

The church says—or should say—concerning what God requires of those whom he has made wealthy only—and all—what the Bible says. Human research and investigation, however thorough, will not suffice. Classical or Marxist economics is not enough, and leads astray if not set in his light. The tenant cannot dictate to the landowner the conditions of his labor or nature of his rent. The tenant—man—can only strive to learn God's rules and to do them lest he face eternal eviction. For if the landowner's will is ignored, his reaction to such rebellion is sure: "What then will the owner of the vineyard do? He will come and kill those tenants and give the vineyard to others" (Mark 12:9). And, indeed, the inexorable passage of time brings new tenants into the vineyard and old tenants to inevitable judgment, where ignorance will be no excuse for disobedience.

What, then, does the church have to say about wealth and its responsibilities?

This question can be answered only on two levels: (1) the teaching of the Scriptures on economic and other matters can be and has been organized into general perspectives, but (2) there is no "Christian economics" that can coerce what the pulpit will speak to the rich—or to the poor. The pulpit is free. Its freedom is guaranteed by obedience to the Word, and to the Word alone. No economics can antecedently prescribe what the Word will say to the rich—or to anyone else—as a text is exegetically applied to the life of the congregation. The sermon is—or ought to be—an adventure. The Word always runs far ahead of where the church is, and the obedient pulpit brings tidings from tomorrow to today. No "Christian" economics dictates content to preaching; it is formulated in the preaching.

We will, therefore, suggest biblical perspectives on the obligations of wealth to its donor, but a living Word can only be spoken into the ear of the rich from the lips of a faithful pastor. Indeed, the Word preached at large to the congregation is particularized in the ear of each who *hears* its syllables. What is said by the pulpit, from the Word, to the wealthy is heard by each in exact proportion to his capacity to hear: "He who has ears, let him hear" (Matt. 11:15). So the Lord expressed the thought we are wishing here to stress, namely that the Word spoken comes alive only in those able truly to "hear" what the Lord is saying on the lips of his ordained servant.

And who, then, comes with ears able to hear?

Only whoever comes desiring, passionately desiring, to have the Word of the Lord addressed to himself: "Seek the LORD your God, you will find him if you look for him with all your heart and with all your soul" (Deut. 4:29).

The Word truly preached will be heard by all truly desirous to know the will of the landowner. He will hear who knows himself a tenant for limited duration, eager to know, because eager to do, the landowner's good pleasure before he returns to demand an accounting of the use made of his good gifts (Matt. 21:33, 40). Such tenants seek out where the Word is faithfully preached, and will hear what the Lord requires of their stewardship.

But he who is rebellious at heart, determined to dispose of "his" wealth as he alone sees fit, will not really hear the Lord's Word even if he forever attend on its proclamation:

> The word of the LORD came to me: "Son of man, you are living among a rebellious people. They have eyes to see but do not see and ears to hear but do not hear, for they are a rebellious people. Therefore, son of man, pack your belongings for exile and in the daytime, as they watch, set out and go from where you are to another place. Perhaps they will understand, though they are a rebellious house." (Ezek. 12:1–3)

Rebels in the vineyard will demand, or devise, their own science of economics, claiming that the Word is economically silent or illiterate—and to them it is.

WHY TO EACH?

Does the preached Word in fact speak to all while being heard (if heard at all) by each?

Indeed, how else can it be? For each of God's image-bearers is unique. If no two snowflakes are ever alike, will two persons ever be? Each of us is a first and only edition. So God acknowledges, and addresses us individually in the Word said to all but particularized by each.

Do you feel that in our mechanized society all slots are alike, and rob everyone of individuality? Anyone can push the broom, bake the pie, tend the machine, occupy the office, farm the land, or teach the class? Maybe so. But that is not the issue when our God-ordained uniqueness is in view. Anyone, or almost anyone, can do your job, but only you can accumulate what doing the job does to the doer. The work may be the same, but each "you" who does the work is unique. And the self that emerges from a lifetime of experience is unlike any other self-made by God. It is not what we *do* that passes into eternity, but who we become by doing. And who we finally are is the living deposit of each day's doing, either in the

light of the Word of God or the twilight of the word of man. God
meets us uniquely because otherwise he would not meet us at all.
He seeks out each of us—by name: "He who has an ear, let him hear
what the Spirit says to the churches. To him who overcomes, I will
give some of the hidden manna. I will also give him a white stone
with a new name written on it, known only to him who receives it"
(Rev. 2:17). Despite appearances to the contrary, life is opportunity
to individuality, and the Word that is addressed to all celebrates the
uniqueness of each by speaking to each where he lives.

The Bible does not permit, therefore, simplistic solutions to
the mystery of riches, such as the following:

> That the rich should give all their wealth away. The Bible
> nowhere prescribes this.
> That the Bible depreciates wealth. On the contrary, the Bible
> equates wealth with divine blessing.
> That the Bible views having great possessions as evidence of
> lack of charity. God rather embraces those to whom he has
> given wealth from the age of the Patriarchs to the present.

The Word speaks uniquely to each of us to ward off such simplistic
exegeses.

ABUSE OF TEXTS

We take note of certain biblical texts often mistakenly employed
to resolve the mystery of wealth:

We have already observed that a rich young man, often called
the rich young ruler, approaches Jesus with a question: "Teacher,
what good thing must I do to get eternal life?" The Lord points
him to the law. The young man claims to have kept the law from
his youth. "Jesus answered, 'If you want to be perfect, go, sell your
possessions and give to the poor, and you will have treasure in
heaven. Then come, follow me'" (Matt. 19:16, 21).

Can only the poor follow him? And is this a mandate laid on
all who are rich: "Go, sell your possessions and give to the poor"?

It would be recklessly simplistic so to interpret the story.

Such total divestiture was not required of Zacchaeus, chief tax
collector of Jericho. Zacchaeus was blessed by the same Lord who

admonished the rich young man to sell all, when Zacchaeus declared: "Here and now I give half of my possessions to the poor" (Luke 19:8).

Sell all, then? Or half? Or . . . ?

We are saying that no generalizations can be derived from simplistic exegesis of selected texts. Clearly, the Lord dealt then as his Word does today, uniquely with each who comes seeking direction for the use of his wealth:

Joseph of Arimathea was "a rich man" (Matt. 27:57–58), who fulfilled prophecy because his riches gave him access to Pilate to secure the body of Jesus for burial in Joseph's new-hewn tomb. Jesus and his disciples were supported by these women "out of their own means" (Luke 8:3). Paul is befriended by the wealthy on his journeys (Acts 16:40). Abraham and all the patriarchs were very rich companions of God, as was King David who was both rich and the prototype of Jesus.

In short, no simplistic inference can be carried over from the advice given the rich young man to the obligations of all the rich who seek to please God. Rather, it becomes obvious that the Word of the Lord addresses, all across history, each of the wealthy in a unique way.

Immediately after the rich young man rejects Jesus' advice, the Lord has the following discussion with his disciples:

> Then Jesus said to his disciples, "I tell you the truth, it is hard for a rich man to enter the kingdom of heaven. Again I tell you, it is easier for a camel to go through the eye of a needle than for a rich man to enter the kingdom of God." When the disciples heard this, they were greatly astonished and asked, "Who then can be saved?" Jesus looked at them and said, "With man this is impossible, but with God all things are possible." (Matt. 19:23–26)

It is easy to infer from this conversation that only those who shrug off all their riches can squeeze through the small gate onto the narrow road that leads to eternal life (Matt. 7:14). An easy, but simplistically mistaken inference.

Why were the disciples "astonished"? Had they hitherto supposed that the rich were guaranteed first entrance upon the kingdom? Therefore, with their exclusion no one at all would make it?

So they seem to say: "Who then [if not the rich] can be saved?" (Matt. 19:25). Perhaps this was their mistaken assumption: first the rich, blessed by God with abundance, and then the poor, less favored from above. "Jesus looked at them," Matthew tells us. Why? Is it a look of surprise? Of disappointment? How little they understand of his coming, and teaching. Can riches ever pry open the gates to the kingdom by being given away? Does wealth unlock the strait gate? Of course not.

Entrance upon the kingdom is quite irrespective of wealth. It is by faith revealed in obedience, also a gift of God: "With man this is impossible, but with God all things are possible" (Matt. 19:26). That is, only God can make the dead soul live and change the alien into a true citizen of the kingdom and a good steward of his blessings.

That the temptations of wealth do indeed threaten entrance upon the kingdom is true. We shall take note of that below. But neither the abundance nor the absence of riches, as such, governs eternal destiny. The soul passes through the eye of the needle by grace, not by selling all it has.

"Do not store up for yourselves treasures on earth" (Matt. 6:19). Is this an admonition against the acquisition of wealth?

It is, if the acquisition is "for yourselves."

It is, then, if the purpose is for saying: "I'll say to myself, 'You have plenty of good things laid up for many years. Take life easy; eat, drink and be merry' (Luke 12:19). Such acquisition characterizes the "fool" (Luke 12:20).

Wealth legitimately acquired may also become capital that, in a free society, has the power to organize human energies into productive enterprise. Goods and services useful to God's world are called into existence by energies assembled and structured for productive efficiency by capital and those characterized by integrity and qualified by talent to accumulate and manage it. Such accumulation of treasure need not be, though it can be, solely "for yourselves." It is not forbidden by Scripture.

Still more, as already pointed out, wealth is power. Would that much more of such power were put to the service of the kingdom by those who have it, and who hear the Word of God addressed to them. The hope of the weak for justice is largely dependent on the power of wealth, and on its influence enlisted for them by the rich who hear the Word of the Lord. The support of kingdom causes depends heavily on the wealthy. Social change in directions pointed by divine law is most readily, and bloodlessly, accomplished through the power of sanctified wealth.

"Son, remember that in your lifetime you received your good things, while Lazarus received bad things, but now he is comforted here and you are in agony" (Luke 16:25).

The speaker is Abraham, who is in heaven comforting Lazarus the poor beggar who lay unattended at rich the rich man's gate and now enjoys the bliss of eternity. He is addressing the rich man who once "was dressed in purple and fine linen and lived in luxury every day" (Luke 16:19), and now, after death, is in hell.

Does this mean an antithesis: rich here, poor there; poor here, rich there? Hardly, for the very Abraham who speaks had been himself very rich, had enjoyed his "good things" on earth, and now appears in heaven.

Time is indeed the vestibule to eternity. The rich man gets where he is by reason of his behavior—or rather, misbehavior—in time. But was hell, then, the "compensation" for his riches?

No, for God himself is the donor of riches. Hell is the rich man's destiny because he accounted God's gifts as solely for his own sensual benefit. He arrives in hell not for what he had but for what he lacked: "If anyone has material possessions and sees his brother in need but has no pity on him, how can the love of God be in him?" (1 John 3:17). Blind of eye, lacking love, the rich man does not see Lazarus' need. Deaf of ear, lacking love, the rich man does not hear Lazarus' weakening pleas. Hard of heart, lacking love, the rich man eats and drinks and makes merry like the fool who says in his heart, "There is no God" (Ps. 14:1) and spends eternity, therefore, in keeping with his profession.

It is lack of love and not God's good gifts to him in his lifetime that determines the rich man's destiny. The Bible does not teach that wealth, in itself, is cursed by compensation with evil after death.

THE MYSTERY

This is the mystery of wealth: that God's good gift can so readily become man's idol. And in the service of the gift instead of the giver man takes the broad road to destruction (Matt. 7:13).

Wealth may come in many ways. Seemingly, it may be by accident or luck, one comes into a fortune. Or by inheritance. Or through hard work, or shrewd investment, or careful saving. Who would know, without the light of the Word, that behind the scenes the ultimate Giver of all riches is God.

Wealth may come in many forms. We concentrate in this chapter on material goods. But there are gifts of talent, of beauty, of warmth of heart, of skills, of qualities of spirit—many that money cannot buy, and some far more rare than money, like artistic abilities. But always the gift can become the god, God's good perverted by man unto his damnation, "They exchanged the truth of God for a lie, and worshiped and served created things rather than the Creator—who is forever praised. Amen" (Rom. 1:25).

The Word, therefore, surrounds wealth with warnings, to which we shall attend. But we stress the point here that these warnings do not include the requirement that he who is blessed with abundance is thereby required to give it all away. There are, we repeat, no such simplistic alternatives for avoiding the burden of responsible use of God's good gifts. The key to responsible employment of wealth comes from the same hand that provides the goods—it is in his inspired Word, given to the church for proclamation to congregation and world. There the mystery of wealth is set in the context of obedience to the giver.

MISTAKEN OPTIONS

Not only are some biblical texts misinterpreted as regards the use of riches, as suggested above, but we believe that what are today called "theologies of liberation" also abuse Scripture for mistaken purposes. We take brief note of this error.

Theology of liberation has followed on theology of revolution, both largely expounded in Central and South America, though with European roots, and both generally developed by Roman Catholic theologians. The motivation is sincere, and the point of departure very real:

Theology of liberation grows out of the observation and experience of human misery and of man's grim inhumanity to man. The awesome misery of the utterly destitute—the mystery of poverty—so common in the Third World provokes pity, rage, and despair. Pity for the helpless, miserable destitute, unable to provide for themselves and, still worse, for their starving and stunted children. Rage against those wealthy enough to help, but coldly, brutally unwilling to do so, and against those utterly indifferent to it all. And despair that so often the church seems so little concerned, so cowardly, and so ineffective. Quite naturally, those who cannot sleep with the moans of misery echoing in their hearts seek license in the Scriptures for revolution and sometimes seek cooperation with Marxists to achieve it. Using the models of Israel's liberation from Egypt—the Exodus—and of Christ's triumph over the power of darkness at Calvary and through the empty tomb—Christ the Liberator—the theology of liberation seeks to take history into its own revolutionary hands.

Starting from the Bible, these theologians sooner or later subdue the Word to their own ultimate designs. Theology of liberation is not obedient response to the abuse of wealth. Consider, for example, this: If we can be appalled, as we should be, by human degradation, how much more must heaven be outraged by man's perversion of God's gifts into instruments of exploitation, how much more must God be anguished by human selfishness and unconcern. We may be sure, therefore, that the Bible has always reckoned seriously with precisely the gross iniquities that drive sensitive souls into plotting revolution. Indeed, the Bible always has: "It is mine to avenge; I will repay" (Deut. 32:35). "For we know him who said, 'It is mine to avenge; I will repay,' and again, 'The Lord will judge his people.'" It is a dreadful thing to fall into the hands of the living God" (Heb. 10:30–31). Time and again, the Word of the Lord assures us that "The Lord is not slow in keeping his promise, as some understand slowness (2 Peter 3:9). The Day of Judgment, far more terrible than any mundane revolution, awaits the merciless:

> Then he will say to those on his left, "Depart from me, you who are cursed, into the eternal fire prepared for the devil and his angels. For I was hungry and you gave me nothing to eat, I was thirsty and you gave me nothing to drink, I was a stranger and you did not invite me in, I needed clothes and you did not clothe me, I was sick and in prison and you did not look after me." "They also will answer, 'Lord, when did we see you hungry or thirsty or a stranger

or needing clothes or sick or in prison, and did not help you?'" "He will reply, 'I tell you the truth, whatever you did not do for one of the least of these, you did not do for me.'" Then they will go away to eternal punishment, but the righteous to eternal life. (Matt. 25:41–46)

The Lord is aware, far more keenly aware than are we, of man's inhumanity to man. His judgment already begins in the unease that the inhumane endure, in the absence of joy that beclouds their seemingly happiest moments, and his judgment concludes in eternal damnation.

What is of crucial importance to the theologian is not revolution but proclamation. Are the rich courageously warned, again and again, that something worse than revolt threatens them if they hoard God's goods against human need, and use God's gifts to exploit God's children: "I tell you, my friends, do not be afraid of those who kill the body and after that can do no more. But I will show you whom you should fear: Fear him who, after the killing of the body, has power to throw you into hell. Yes, I tell you, fear him" (Luke 12:4–5). That is, fear God. Let the church so warn mankind:

You are storing up wrath against yourself for the day of God's wrath, when his righteous judgment will be revealed. God "will give to each person according to what he has done." To those who by persistence in doing good seek glory, honor and immortality, he will give eternal life. But for those who are self-seeking and who reject the truth and follow evil, there will be wrath and anger. (Rom. 2:5–8)

Let theologians demand such preaching.

Political revolution, which seeks freedom for proclamation and for obedience according to conscience, is *justified* by Scripture, and has given the Western world the liberties we now enjoy. But *economic* revolution, along Marxist lines, has enthroned tyranny wherever it has been successful, and has destroyed the freedom of preaching without which a society becomes its own prison. Marxist revolution has sometimes provided bread at the expense of liberty, but the world observes that the Solzhenitsyns who speak for multitudes declare "that man does not live on bread alone but on every word that comes from the mouth of the LORD" (Deut. 8:3), quoted by Christ against the Devil, (Matt. 4:4). Theology of liberation, so long as it substitutes economic for political Exodus, only points to the substitution of one tyranny for another.

Finally, theology of liberation via Marxist revolt assumes that evil has an explanation and, therefore, a rational cure. This is not a biblical, but rather a secular premise. Evil surfaces in human exploitation and callous greed. Evil tramples on the destitute in the persons of the greedy. But evil is without explanation. Evil has parentage—the Evil One—but no ground. Evil responds to no "why" or "wherefore." Hard heart, blind eye, deaf ear—the origin of these is hidden in "the secret power of lawlessness" (2 Thess. 2:7). The Bible assigns no cause for human depravity that may be isolated by social or psychological or economic relationships and then assumes that abolition of such relationships cures evil at its source. The dimensions of this mistake are evident in the crop of evil that Communist tyranny so abundantly produced.

The Bible knows but one source of man's inhumanity to man. It is the depraved human heart. And the Bible knows but one cure for depraved hearts—the indwelling of Christ, by way of his Word, which makes new what was depraved: "Therefore, if anyone is in Christ, he is a new creation; the old has gone, the new has come!" (2 Cor. 5:17).

We are not endorsing the substitution of "faith" for obedience or the preaching of heaven as substitute for social justice. We are saying that the Bible sets the Word of God, faithfully and fully and courageously preached, in the fore of man's pursuit of social righteousness. The world may give up on the Word of God and turn to the words of Marx. But the church can never forget that the only lastingly liberating power available to man in history is the Bible truly preached:

> As the rain and the snow
>   come down from heaven,
> and do not return to it
>   without watering the earth
> and making it bud and flourish,

> so that it yields seed for the sower
> and bread for the eater,
> so is my word that goes out from my mouth:
> It will not return to me empty,
> but will accomplish what I desire
> and achieve the purpose for which I sent it.
>
> —Isa. 55:10–11

This is the Word of the Lord. "Simon Peter answered him, 'Lord, to whom shall we go? You have the words of eternal life'" (John 6:68). To those who despair of the Word's power to effect social change, there is the Lord's warning: "There is a judge for the one who rejects me and does not accept my words; that very word which I spoke will condemn him at the last day" (John 12:48).

Either the church and her theologians trust the power of the Word to transform social evil, or that Word will on the last day judge the church herself for apostasy.

We therefore believe that the Word fearlessly preached, from every pulpit free to speak it, is far more productive of social righteousness than the threat or even the success of Marxist revolt.

Moreover, we believe that the Exodus is not the symbol of successful *economic* rebellion. It was the passage from bondage to the opportunity freely to serve Jehovah. The Exodus is a model for political, but not for economic, revolution. The goal of the Exodus is the right to worship: "Then say to Pharaoh, 'This is what the LORD says: Israel is my firstborn son, and I told you, "Let my son go, so he may worship me." (Ex. 4:22–23). And the Exodus in time produces the proclamation: "proclaim liberty throughout the land to all its inhabitants" (Lev. 25:10). To such revolution, the kind that gave democracy to one country after another in the West after the Reformation, the Bible lends support. And for such revolution the Exodus serves as a model, as does the Christ who liberates us also from Egyptian bondage, that we may freely serve him.

For the path out of Egypt leads directly to Sinai where God reveals why he liberates his people, then and now: "I am the LORD your God, who brought you out of Egypt, out of the land of slavery. "You shall have no other gods before me" (Ex. 20:2–3).

We observe, then, that theology of liberation is not the Bible's approach to resolving the obligation of riches to the God who gives them. At the same time, we believe that the Bible does endorse political revolution where it is necessary to secure freedom of the pulpit and liberty of obedience according to conscience.

What, then, is the Bible's approach to man and his wealth?

BIBLICAL PERSPECTIVES—GENERAL

What the Lord requires of each of his children as return on his gifts to them will be specifically heard, we have observed, by each in the Spirit-guided conjunction of Word proclaimed, of willing ear, and in the light of circumstances peculiar to each listener.

The Bible does provide certain perspectives that everyone can employ for teaching themselves and helping their congregation see the obligations of wealth. First, general perspectives such as the following:

The Christian must seek to put himself and all his time, talents, and goods at God's disposal. Not at God's disposal as we wish or think that to be, but at God's disposal as he graciously reveals his will in his Word. This is the true believer's response to the first of the Great Commandments: "Love the Lord your God with all your heart and with all your soul and with all your strength and with all your mind" (Luke 10:27; Deut. 6:5). To love God is to obey him. The believer obeys; the obedient believe. Of this, rich Abraham is prime example. Thus to love God according to the first commandment is deliberately to put oneself and all one has under his directives as revealed in his Word. The wealthy who turn to the church for guidance from the Scriptures as to appropriate use of their goods, set themselves in the right posture for doing good stewardship.

A parallel, in the church, of such docility—teachableness—appears in the relationship between the preaching and the Word. The obedient pulpit serves the inspired text even as the preacher employs his own words to expound and apply it. "He who listens to you," the Lord says of such preaching, "listens to me" (Luke 10:16). How do human words become God's? By *obedience* to the text. The preacher whose sole desire is to obey the Word of the Lord as he shapes his thoughts, and phrases his sentences, attains this awesome authority: What he says, in obedience to the text, God in Christ says. Similarly, in close parallel, the believer who submits what he *does* with his wealth to governance by the Word may know that what *he* does God is doing with, and through, him. This is obedience to the first Great Commandment.

A second general biblical perspective is opened by the second of the Great Commandments: "Love your neighbor as yourself" (Luke 10:27; Lev. 19:18). Obedience to God results in service to neighbor. Love of God is authenticated by love for man. It is striking that Paul sets this priority in his great hymn to love in the first letter to Corinth: First love, that is to say, the will to obey the Word, and then all else; but, lacking love, all else too becomes nothing: "If I give all I possess to the poor and surrender my body to the flames, but have not love, I gain nothing" (1 Cor. 13:3).

The Word of God works, as it were, by indirection. It achieves one end by seeming to aim at another. Seeking the open hand and generous heart, the Word points us to love. Given love, all else follows; lacking love, no good can come. Therefore, the apostle concludes: "Follow the way of love" (1 Cor. 14:1). Therefore all that is commanded us in the Law is summed up in *love*. The church that preaches love, as duty to obey rather than as warmth of emotion, is a church where the fruits of love will be achieved as by-product.

The two Great Commandments, therefore, are the general biblical guidelines for the proper use of all God's gifts.

BIBLICAL PERSPECTIVES—SPECIFIC

In the context of the Commandments, the Bible lays down more specific perspectives on the proper use of wealth:

There are repeated warnings against letting possessions become masters rather than remaining servants:

First, "No one can serve two masters. Either he will hate the one and love the other, or he will be devoted to the one and despise the other. You cannot serve both God and Money" (Matt. 6:24).

Man is capable of two loves, two servitudes, but not at the same time. He can love, that is obey, God in the service of neighbor, or he can love gold in the service of self. The Word of the Lord comes to oblige us to choose, not only once but day after day: "See, I am setting before you today a blessing and a curse—the blessing if you obey the commands of the LORD your God that I am giving you today; the curse if you disobey the commands of the LORD your God and turn from the way that I command you today by following other gods, which you have not known" (Deut. 11:26–28).

The same hand may grasp with greed *and* give a smattering away, but the heart can only serve one master: God or self. Moses puts the alternatives again:

> This day I call heaven and earth as witnesses against you that I have set before you life and death, blessings and curses. Now choose life, so that you and your children may live and that you may love the LORD your God, listen to his voice, and hold fast to him. For the LORD is your life, and he will give you many years in the land he swore to give to your fathers, Abraham, Isaac and Jacob. (Deut. 30:19–20)

Think not that this choice was only presented, ages ago, to people long since gone from the face of the earth. It is precisely the choice set before us now, and always: "Now choose life". Surrender yourself and all you have to the will of the Lord as revealed in his Word. For not to serve him *is* to serve the adversary. The heart can have but one guiding star. There is no dual citizenship as between the kingdom of heaven and . . . another.

Second, riches not put to God's disposal threaten the very roots of the spiritual life. In his parable of the sower, Christ teaches that the Word once received may yet be choked out by "the worries of this life and the deceitfulness of wealth" (Matt. 13:22). Wealth does not itself stand as neutral over against the soul. What is not freely committed to control by the Word quickly becomes enemy to the Word, and threatens to throttle the voice of the Lord and darken the light of his revelation. Enemies of obedience are the fingers of greed and the showy tinsel of affluence.

Third, Paul goes so far as to charge that "For the love of money is a root of all kinds of evil" (1 Tim. 6:10). Here, as elsewhere, the Scripture is not condemning wealth as such. It is the *love* of money that is condemned. For love always makes of its object an end in itself. Fourth, the Wisdom of Proverbs reinforces the same truth: "Do not wear yourself out to get rich; have the wisdom to show restraint" (Prov. 23:4). Once again, warned against here is the pursuit of wealth as an end in itself, or as solely the means of gratifying one's own selfish desires.

Fifth, in summary, biblical passages such as these, which might be multiplied, establish perspectives on wealth in terms of two absolute alternatives: (1) either we place our goods of all kinds at God's disposal under his Word, or (2) these good gifts become an intolerable burden weighting the soul toward hell and hardening the heart against all appeals from the needy.

The Bible also suggests perspectives on specific economic relationships. We instance but an illustrative few:

Pay wages promptly and in full: "Look. The wages you failed to pay the workmen who mowed your fields are crying out against you. The cries of the harvesters have reached the ears of the Lord Almighty" (James 5:4). This admonition of the Lord's Word is as timely today as when the apostle penned it. All employers owe it obedience in terms of their own business affairs.

Be generous: "When you reap the harvest of your land, do not reap to the very edges of your field or gather the gleanings of your harvest. Do not go over your vineyard a second time or pick up the grapes that have fallen. Leave them for the poor and the alien. I am the LORD your God" (Lev. 19:9). Economic circumstances change, but God does not. Though he has every *legal* right to do so, the owner or employer is *not* to extract every penny he can— remember the needs of those employed by you, or within reach of your generosity.

Be scrupulously honest: "Do not use dishonest standards when measuring length, weight or quantity. Use honest scales and honest weights, an honest *ephahd* and an honest *hin*. I am the LORD your God, who brought you out of Egypt" (Lev. 19:35–36). The same Lord our God has brought us, too, in Christ, out of Egyptian bondage to Satan, to ourselves, and to our possessions. In Egypt anything goes but not among those for whom the Lord is God. Among them, there must be absolute integrity in every transaction, including refusal to buy cheap and sell dear, if no value be added in between.

Pay labor what it is worth: "I will be quick to testify against sorcerers, adulterers and perjurers, against those who defraud laborers of their wages, who oppress the widows and the fatherless" (Mal. 3:5). Do not take advantage of the defenseless in your employ. Do not league with necessity to drive hard bargains, pay starvation wages, or demand overtime without remuneration.

Avoid usury: "Do not charge your brother interest, whether on money or food or anything else that may earn interest" (Deut. 23:19). The church since the late middle ages has distinguished between the right to take interest on commercial loans, which are not in view here, and taking interest on loans made to a neighbor in his necessity. Risk capital owes the payment of interest. The needy brother, if he cannot pay, may not be threatened for either interest or even the loan itself. Such is the biblical teaching.

Summary: Thoroughly and courageously preached, the Bible opens compelling perspectives on the economic relationships that produce wealth, and into which wealth enters. It is easy to see that these texts, and many that might be added to them, simply focus on particular relationships the light shed by the obligation to love. Or, to put it another way, biblical economics specifies what the Lord requires by saying: "So in everything, do to others what you would have them do to you, for this sums up the Law and the Prophets" (Matt. 7:12).

THE BIBLICAL SUMMARY

What the Bible teaches concerning the obligations imposed by God in the gift of riches is summed up by Paul in words that explain themselves:

> Command those who are rich in this present world not to be arrogant nor to put their hope in wealth, which is so uncertain, but to put their hope in God, who richly provides us with everything for our enjoyment. Command them to do good, to be rich in good deeds, and to be generous and willing to share. In this way they will lay up treasure for themselves as a firm foundation for the coming age, so that they may take hold of the life that is truly life. (1 Tim. 6:17–19)

This summary of the Bible's perspectives on wealth should be preached, and pondered, and obeyed in the church of Jesus Christ.

TWIN MYSTERIES: CONCLUDING OBSERVATIONS

The aim of Christianity is fellowship with God.

The conditions for entering upon such fellowship are prescribed by the Holy Scriptures: "Jesus replied, 'If anyone loves me, he will obey my teaching. My Father will love him, and we will come to him and make our home with him'" (John 14:23).

God gives us life and time for the sole purpose of beginning a fellowship with him that will be consummated in eternity: "And I heard a loud voice from the throne saying, 'Now the dwelling of God is with men, and he will live with them. They will be his people, and God himself will be with them and be their God'" (Rev. 21:3).

God adds to life and time all other gifts of talent and goods, and provides in his Word instructions for making these into means for facilitating fellowship with him. Mysteriously, and without explanation, he blesses many with poverty and some with riches. In both instances, God's design for promoting our fellowship with him through the right use of his gifts may be frustrated by our disobedient use of them.

The church has equal obligation to preach and teach the Word to poor and rich alike: "Hear this, all you peoples; listen, all who live in this world, both low and high, rich and poor alike" (Ps. 49:1–2). And this, as regards riches and poverty, is the substance of the church's teaching: "The LORD gave and the LORD has taken away; may the name of the LORD be praised" (Job 1:21). "Your ears will hear a voice behind you, saying, "This is the way; walk in it"" (Isa. 30:21).

In this light we make the following observations:

It is as difficult for the rich to acknowledge that all their possessions are God's gifts as it is for the poor to recognize that their want is God's provision. Preaching both, and teaching them, will not be popular.

Materialism is as likely to characterize the poor as the rich—the one longing to acquire riches, and the other determined to hoard them.

Materialism may also characterize social reformers, even "Christian" social reformers, whose goals in practice often decline to crassly economic levels.

A noisy, pretentious concern for the poor may cloak a deep envy of the rich.

Intellectual reformers do not hesitate to use the poor as a lever on the public conscience, not so much to alleviate poverty in itself as to attain their own manipulative ends. Unlike some child psychologists, the Bible never hesitates to motivate behavior by promise of reward. Christ offers the rich young man what should have been a tempting alternative: "Sell everything you have and give to the poor, and you will have treasure in heaven" (Luke 18:22). Surrender the temporal, and acquire the eternal—who offers a better bargain, and promises greater reward? It is some indication of the blindness induced by riches that this probably shrewd businessman turned the Lord down. But the Word promises reward, both temporal and eternal, for obedience. So should the church. The Bible also, of course, guarantees grim "reward" for disobedience, especially on the Day of Judgment, and no one lays more emphasis on that than our Lord himself.

Our own materialism tempts us to interpret every biblical reference to riches and to poverty in terms of material goods. It is evident, however, that the Word uses both "rich" and "poor" with far broader connotation, such as:

First, the biblical "poor" are those who know that their most basic needs for time and eternity *cannot* be met short of the Gospel, as the Bible presents the Gospel—namely, the power of God to make disciples out of rebels. These, whatever their material wealth, are the true poor to whom "the good news is preached to the poor" (Luke 7:22) and who gladly surrender all they have to God's service (like the man who commits all he has to buying a field where the treasure is hidden—Matt. 13:44). Such "poor" are those who, because they know their own emptiness (however much they have in the ways of goods), are filled "with good things" by the birth of the Lord (as Mary sings in her "magnificat," Luke 1:53). Such "poor" are those to whom "the kingdom of God" belongs because they know that God alone can give citizenship in that kingdom (Luke 6:20). These "poor" may be destitute or may be blessed in material possession, but their poverty is the only gateway to the "true riches" (Luke 16:11). Only God really knows who among us are such "poor," though their fellowship with him will be suggested by their eagerness to put themselves and all they have at the disposal of his Word. The goal of the church, in this context, is to alert us all to our *real* poverty.

Second, conversely, the Bible often derides the "rich" for their blindness, meaning those who are unaware of needs more profound than earthly goods can supply. These "rich" may possess great measures of wealth and talent, but they may also be materially destitute and greedily seeking riches—in either case their trust is in riches or power or acclaim and their ambition is to acquire them. These are the "rich" sent "away empty" from the birth of Jesus, like those who filled the inn that first Christmas Eve and ignored the stable (Luke 1:53). These are the rich who are castigated by the prophets, warned by the Lord, and condemned by the apostles, for putting God's gifts to their own service and trusting in the creature rather than in the Creator.

Third, unless the Christian bears these biblical uses of the terms *poor* and *rich* well in mind, he is apt to confuse the instruction that the Word gives on wealth and poverty. The Bible does, indeed, speak directly to riches and poverty as such. Each reference in the Scriptures must be carefully tested as to what riches and which poverty are being discussed.

We conclude these observations with two illustrations of how a text may be confused by imposing materialistic interpretation on its terms:

First, one of the most stringent biblical admonitions concerning possessions occurs in Matthew's account of Sermon on the Mount: "So do not worry, saying, 'What shall we eat?' or 'What shall we drink?' or 'What shall we wear?' For the pagans run after all these things, and your heavenly Father knows that you need them. But seek first his kingdom and his righteousness, and all these things will be given to you as well" (Matt. 6:31–33).

Much is written about the kingdom of heaven. What does it mean to seek it first? And how, then, will food, drink, and clothing come tumbling after?

Quite simply, as is evident by definition, a kingdom exists where citizens swear allegiance to a king and undertake to obey his laws. All those who profess fidelity to God as their King and strive as loyal citizens to do his will constitute the kingdom of heaven in its temporal manifestation. Citizenship in God's kingdom is not in conflict with political allegiance to any state that does not restrict liberty of worship and conscience. Indeed, the Christian is required by God to be a good citizen of such a nation. This is what the Lord implies by telling Pilate, "My kingdom is not of this world" (John 18:36). Citizens of his kingdom are interspersed among all nations. There is not, and cannot be, a geographical kingdom of heaven located among the world countries. God's kingdom has no geography—and expands across all geography.

To seek, then, the righteousness of God's kingdom means simply to do God's will with all our might and all our gifts and talents. And will this, then, bring down a flood of riches? Yes, if it be remembered, now, that "riches" come in far more forms than just the material. But the Lord is speaking, in the text, directly to material goods: food, drink, clothing. How are these "ours" by first seeking the kingdom's righteousness? Because all goods are, as it were, not really ours but simply on lease to us from the giver *until we put them to his service*. Goods kept wholly for ourselves never do, really, pass from temporal lease to permanent possession. None of these is invested in heaven for permanent possession. We get lasting ownership only of those gifts we put to work here for the kingdom, according to the King's Word: "But seek first his kingdom and his righteousness, and all these things will be given to you as well" (Matt. 6:33).

Second, "Sell your possessions and give to the poor. Provide purses for yourselves that will not wear out, a treasure in heaven that will not be exhausted, where no thief comes near and no moth destroys" (Luke 12:33).

Some moralists call this a counsel of perfection. We think of it as fitting into the biblical perspectives we have been outlining.

It is obvious on reflection that by no means all of God's gifts to us can literally be sold. Only material possessions can. Moreover, many of God's most obedient servants, like the Patriarchs, did not divest themselves of all their material goods. What, then, is meant here by "sell your possessions"?

To sell is to transfer title, done in consideration of a certain return. When, in consideration of a certain need, we place goods at the disposal of another, or place our time and talents in the service of another in love, we do fulfill the condition of the Lord's command to "sell" possessions. The purpose of goods is to serve.

When we put the power lent us by great possessions into the service of justice benefitting those who need justice, this is as surely "selling" our goods as is turning them into money. Yes, let those who are influential so "sell" their possessions for the benefit of the needy. They will discover that the promise of reward is sure: "a treasure in the heavens that does not fail."

A final word: The Bible takes for granted that we know from experience how much "rich" and "poor" measure. The Word gives no definition of either. We know that the poor in a wealthy nation may be rich by contrast to the destitute in a deprived nation. We could stumble long and frustrate action indefinitely by demanding a definition of "rich" and "poor" before putting ourselves and our gifts at God's command.

The needy become visible, not by definition but to the eye seeking out opportunities for obedience. Whoever seeks fellowship with God by finding him where service can be rendered to man will find the needy without ever defining them.

He or she is poor, right now, who needs something that another could give. He or she is rich, right now, who has something another needs. Often such needs can be measured, and met, in terms of material goods. As often, or perhaps oftener, human needs cry out for other forms of wealth, in compassion, concern, human interest, time, companionship, a smile, a word, a note, a call, a hand, a ride, a prayer. . . . By "selling" these, the kingdom is formed.

There are certain parables written in the Scriptures just to teach stewardship.

THE GOOD SAMARITAN: AWARE, CARE, SHARE

The parable of the Good Samaritan is familiar. A man was traveling from Jerusalem to Jericho. He is fallen upon by thieves who stripped and beat him and left him lying at the roadside half dead. A priest passed by, saw the victim, and crossed over to avoid him. So did a Levite. But a Samaritan, stranger to the victim by race and religion, saw him and had compassion on him. He bound up the man's wounds, put him on his beast, took him to an inn, and paid in advance for his care and keeping.

"Which of these three do you think," the Lord asks, "was a neighbor to the man who fell into the hands of robbers?" On hearing the answer, "The one who had mercy on him," Jesus said, "Go and do likewise" (Luke 10:25–37).

First, one of the perpetual problems that Christians face is illumined here. Between the Samaritan and the victim there was no kinship of religion or community. Yet Jesus clearly commands just this kind of mercy. All Christians are obliged to reach out in care and concern and practical assistance to all those about them who are in need.

Second, this parable highlights three attitudes that believers must cultivate.

Are You Aware?

Three people passed by the man lying beaten along the roadside. No doubt all three saw him there, but two of them were not aware, somehow, that here was human need crying out for their help. Perhaps they were too busy with their own affairs, or with those of formal service to God. Whatever the explanation, they were not aware.

It is a question that Christians must persistently put to themselves, both individually and in their meetings together: Are we aware of the needs surrounding us? Do we see with the eye of love what cries out for our attention? In fact, do we want to see need and hear cries of distress?

Do You Care?

Two of those who passed by the man at the roadside may have been aware but did not care. They felt no compulsion to assist. They heard no mandate of conscience. They declined to be neighbors.

From becoming aware to starting to care can be a difficult step. All kinds of reasons might be advanced why needs of which we have reluctantly become aware cannot really be met.

The parable passes no judgment on the two who either were not aware or did not care. It only pronounces blessing on the one who did. The inference is unmistakable, and the command reinforces it: God requires caring—a caring that overcomes whatever obstacles may be posed against service.

Will You Share?

The Lord has only one answer to this question: "Go and do likewise!"

Those who are of God must be neighbors to any who are in need of whatever God has given them to share with others. Christians must be good stewards.

THE VINEYARD: FOR THOSE WHO DO NOT CARE

The prophet Isaiah tells of a vineyard on a fertile hillside: Its owner "dug it up and cleared it of stones and planted it with the choicest vines. Then he looked for a crop of good grapes, but it yielded only bad fruit." In his disappointment, he declares: "I will make it a wasteland, neither pruned nor cultivated, and briers and thorns will grow there" (Isa. 5:1–6).

The same theme is taken up by our Lord and reported in three of the Gospels (Matt. 21:33–46; Mark 12:1–12; Luke 20:9–19).

In each instance, it is clear that by the vineyard is meant the church. For her the Lord has done all that can be done to insure the fruits of obedience and service. He has planted. He has preserved. He has sent prophets and teachers to instruct in his ways. He has given his Son that the guilt of the church might be washed away. What then does he ask of us? The obedience summed up in the love of God and neighbor.

It is our duty to distribute the fruit of the vineyard to those in need. The role of the vineyard is to provide fruit for such distribution. And the absence of such stewardship is no little thing. The terrible punishment foretold by Isaiah did fall on fruitless Israel and does fall on fruitless "Christians" throughout history: "Do not be deceived: God cannot be mocked. A man reaps what he sows. The one who sows to please his sinful nature, from that nature will reap destruction; the one who sows to please the Spirit, from the Spirit will reap eternal life" (Gal. 6:7–8).

Hear then the conclusion of the matter, an admonition to the church and mandate to the individual: "Let us not become weary in doing good, for at the proper time we will reap a harvest if we do not give up. Therefore, as we have opportunity, let us do good to all people, especially to those who belong to the family of believers" (Gal. 6:9–10). "God 'will give to each person according to what he has done.' To those who by persistence in doing good seek glory, honor and immortality, he will give eternal life. But for those who are self-seeking and who reject the truth and follow evil, there will be wrath and anger" (Rom. 2:6–8).

THE GOOD SAMARITAN: ANOTHER LOOK

A man traveling from Jerusalem to Jericho falls among thieves. They rob and beat him, leaving him half dead at the roadside.

A priest hurries by, perhaps late for the time of sacrifice. He ignores the bloody figure in the ditch. So does a Levite who next comes by. Two religious professionals neglect the love of neighbor that they profess.

But a stranger, a Samaritan, one of a people alien to the beaten man, pauses, bends to dress the man's wounds, hoists him on his donkey, takes him to an inn, and pays in advance for his care. All this is a story told 'round the world: the parable of the Good Samaritan (Luke 10:25–37), as recounted, also, above.

Has it become so familiar that you do not notice that the question that provoked the parable is not the question that our Lord answers?

The discussion began over eternal life. How shall we inherit that most desirable of all blessings? A lawyer wants to know: "What must I do to inherit eternal life?"

Jesus asks him what the Law requires, and the lawyer knows: "Love the Lord your God with all your heart; and, love your neighbor as yourself."

Jesus commends his answer and adds, "Do this and you will live."

"But he wanted to justify himself, so he asked Jesus, 'And who is my neighbor?'" This is strange language. How "justify himself"? For what?

We know from our own experience. What we mean to justify by complicating the definition of "neighbor" is our own behavior in doing what the priest and the Levite did. We mean to leave the definition of "neighbor" so vague as to justify passing by many who lie beaten on life's roadsides. And we mean to substitute the delight of talk for the difficulties of obedience. The lawyer indeed means to "justify" himself—and us.

This then is the question shrewdly posed for the afternoon's leisurely exploration with the "Teacher": Just who is my neighbor? That is, who is the one I must love as I do myself? Not everyone, surely? Least of all a stranger or alien? By what marks shall I know him? Puzzles enough for an endless delay in actualizing love.

But the Lord brushes such speculation aside. He is a teacher who aims at action: "Do this and you will live."

After telling the immortal story, Jesus quietly rephrases the lawyer's question. He does not say, "There, now you see who your neighbor is—not the priest, not the Levite, but the beaten stranger."

No, he rephrases the question in a way that can no longer be endlessly refined, disputed, and thus evaded: "Which of these three do you think was a neighbor to the man who fell into the hands of robbers?"

What was to be a long afternoon's idle talk ended abruptly. The lawyer was obliged to say: "The one who had mercy on him."

And the clever would-be disputant was then dismissed with a curt, "Go and do likewise"! Why waste time discussing how we will know who our neighbor is? Just go and be "neighbor" to someone, to anyone, in need. Let the needy find his neighbor in you.

Drop the talk. Cut the chatter. Take God's gifts of time, money, goods, talents, counsel, a listening ear, a helping hand . . . out there where someone can use them.

To love a neighbor as yourself means simply to *be* a neighbor whenever and wherever you can.

Who is the neighbor?

Each of us is—or ought to be.

GIVE AND FORGIVE

"Give us today our daily bread. Forgive us our debts, as we also have forgiven our debtors" (Matt. 6:11–12).

A parable may be drawn from these familiar lines, taken from the prayer that the Lord instructs all Christians to use: "This, then, is how you should pray" (Matt. 6:9).

Notice the play on words: "give" but "forgive."

The prefix *for* has the force of "not" here, of negation, of blotting out. We are asking God to "give" us all that we need for daily life, but "not" to give us the debit against our account that such giving lays upon us. *Give* us our bread, we pray, but *not* the debt that taking it should put on us: give and forgive.

We need from God all that sustains daily life—all that makes it comfortable and enables us to do our work and enjoy our play. The Lord invites us to ask "Our Father" for all this, and he commonly gives far more than we know how to ask. This is why the prayer is made very simple: "daily bread" covers the needs we know and countless others of which we are completely unaware.

This we do know, or should: We are far from using all his gifts in his required service, namely in the loving of our neighbors as ourselves. The debt we incur by accepting his gifts must be forgiven at once: We pray "give" and "forgive" in the same breath.

Too much of what we are asking for will end up on the altar of self—or even of Satan.

The words flow easily enough . . . give . . . forgive. Who knows how often we have mouthed them?

But the Lord, whose prayer this is, obliges us to take upon ourselves a pledge: "as we also have forgiven our debtors."

And who are they?

They must be those who bear the same relationship to us that we bear to God: recipients of "daily bread" at our hand.

We acquire "debtors" just as God acquires them, by doing good. We put others in debt to us by doing for them what we ask God to do for us: Give us what we need as we give others what they need.

The command to "love your neighbor as yourself" means to make debtors. How else shall we be able to keep our part of the prayer's pledge, "as we also have forgiven our debtors"?

Two obligations are implied by the pledge we say so readily: (1) that we make debtors through our generosity, and (2) that we exact no compensation from them in return, not even thanks or appreciation.

Then we can pray: "Forgive us our debts, as we also have forgiven our debtors."

The Lord stresses this relationship: "Forgive, and you will be forgiven" (Luke 6:37). The Lord emphasizes this solemn truth in another familiar story that follows.

SIMON'S SURPRISE

Simon the Pharisee invited the "Teacher" to dinner. Whatever he may have expected in the way of good talk, he certainly did not anticipate what he was going to hear about himself (Luke 7:36–50).

The Lord came to dinner.

While he was sitting at the table, "a woman who had lived a sinful life" slipped in among the guests. Saying nothing, "She began to wet his feet with her tears. Then she wiped them with her hair, kissed them and poured perfume on them" that she had brought with her.

The Pharisee was disappointed. He thought that he had invited a "prophet" to be his guest, but this "Teacher" was apparently unaware of how unsavory was the character who as touching him. A wasted evening after all, Simon was probably thinking, for, "If this man were a prophet, he would know who is touching him and what kind of woman she is—that she is a sinner."

Thus will men prescribe how God ought to behave—if only he were as "wise" as we are in our own sight.

But the Teacher was more of a prophet than Simon could possibly have surmised, and he breaks into Simon's reverie with what will become a scathing rebuke: "Simon, I have something to tell you."

Unaware of what lies ahead, Simon asks, "Tell me, teacher."

And the Lord begins to talk of debts and debtors—the theme we have just considered in the Lord's Prayer.

"Two men owed money to a certain moneylender. One owed him five hundred *denarii*, and the other fifty. Neither of them had the money to pay him back, so he canceled the debts of both. Now which of them will love him more?"

Like the lawyer asking, "And who is my neighbor?" Simon walks into the trap from which there will be no escape. He says, "I suppose the one who had the bigger debt canceled."

Whereupon Jesus lists the ways in which the woman had served him in courtesies that Simon had callously neglected: Simon had not given him, as custom required, water to wash his feet before dinner—the woman had supplied the lack with her tears. Simon had greeted him with no kiss, as courtesy required—the woman had kissed his feet. Simon had provided no oil with which he might groom his hair and beard—the woman had anointed his feet with ointment.

She had, in short, shown him much love; Simon very little.

But the love we show reflects the love we have received. The debts we create by giving, and then forgive, measure our debts against God that he has graciously forgiven: "Therefore, I tell you, her many sins have been forgiven—for she loved much. But he who has been forgiven little loves little."

Those who create few debtors by acts of love are, in fact, forgiven few of the immense range of debts we owe the Father. An absence of love for the neighbor betrays an absence of entrance on the forgiving love of God.

The believer has a dual concern in all of his efforts to steward his blessing: (1) as God commands, the needy shall be satisfied with the gifts that he has entrusted to the stewardship of others for this purpose, and (2) a generous heart testifies to a forgiven sinner, while a stingy heart betrays its own hardness.

APPRENTICESHIP CHRISTIANITY

> I am the way and the truth and the life. No one comes to the Father except through me. (John 14:6)

Have you ever wondered why the Lord puts this order—way, truth, life—on his answer to Thomas' question?

The Lord had said to his disciples that he was going away. In John 14:5, Thomas speaks for them all in asking: "Lord, we don't know where you are going, so how can we know the way?"

Thomas thought that knowing comes first, and then going the right way follows. So, often, do we. A few years ago a book based on this text was issued by several authors who tried to improve on the Lord's teaching method by revising his order: They made it into, "the truth, the way, and the life." However, that is not what the Lord says, and it is not, therefore, what he means. Jesus is talking about apprenticeship Christianity, where doing precedes understanding.

Our Lord's heavenly Father destined him to be raised in a carpenter's family. So, at least, is the tradition regarding Joseph. Carpentry, like most skills, can be talked about endlessly but is really learned only by doing. Oh yes, the master carpenter tells the apprentice what to do, but the apprentice comes to knowing carpentry only by doing it. That makes all the difference between a sagging door hung by a novice and a neatly fitted one hung by a craftsman. The novice knows *about* carpentry; the master *knows* carpentry. This is true about most of living. First the doing, under guidance, and then the understanding. First the way; then the truth.

Remember that our Lord was not predestined by his Father to birth where we might have expected him, say into Herod's palace or a Scribe's scholarly abode. He was born, by divine design, into a laboring man's dwelling. He draws, in all his teaching, on examples taken from every man's daily life.

It is entirely in keeping with his upbringing by Joseph and Mary, according to God's predestined intent, that our Lord precedes understanding with doing. He sets the *way* before the truth. His hermeneutic (that is, his method of interpretation and understanding) is an apprenticeship hermeneutic. And it is every man's hermeneutic. Open to all who believe. Not reserved for the learned, or the wealthy, or the powerful, or the famous. Quite the opposite, really: "The large crowd listened to him with delight" (Mark 12:37). To all who, like Jesus' own disciples, learned their work by doing it, he quite naturally would say: First the way, then the truth of understanding, and in these the true life—apprenticeship Christianity.

Oh yes, like the master craftsman, the Lord offers guidance for finding the right way. The Psalmist pointed that out centuries ago: "Your word is a lamp to my feet and a light for my path" (Ps. 119:105). Peter said it, too: "Lord, to whom shall we go? You have the words of eternal life" (John 6:68).

The Lord's word order is fundamental: First the way; then the truth grasped by our understanding; and, in these, the discovery of new life: "I am the way and the truth and the life."

One more thing Christians must observe: Jesus says, "I am."

We never seek or walk the way alone. He is the very Word that sheds light on the path: "In the beginning was the Word, and the Word was with God, and the Word was God. In him was life, and that life was the light of men" (John 1:1, 4). Those who come to understand the Word by doing it on the way of, and to, life, find that he has been joined with them on the way: "If anyone loves me, he will obey my teaching. My Father will love him, and we will come to him and make our home with him" (John 14:23). This blessed discovery of the presence of Jesus and his Father in the Word that guides our feet along the way is no doubt what "understanding" the truth really means. That is, we understand the Word by standing under the Word as it illumines our path. And in such standing under we have Jesus as companion, for he too came to walk the way set by his Father's will: "I seek not to please myself but him who sent me" (John 5:30).

Those who walk the way of obedience, that is the way of love to God and for neighbor made manifest in deeds, discover that Jesus Christ is, indeed, the way, the truth, and the life: "I have been crucified with Christ and I no longer live, but Christ lives in me. The life I live in the body, I live by faith in the Son of God, who loved me and gave himself for me" (Gal. 2:20).

PROGRESS FOLLOWS VISION

Those who aspire to participate in the Lord's designs for his church must dream a little and must extend their reach beyond their grasp. Look up. Look around. Look ahead. Your office is an active function of a body that is in league with the most progressive force in history—the power of the risen Lord: "I pray also that the eyes of your heart may be enlightened in order that you may know the hope to which he has called you, the riches of his glorious inheritance in the saints, and his incomparably great power for us who believe" (Eph. 1:18–19).

Vision taps that power, when it is vision bent on obedience to the head of the church, whom God raised from the dead, "and seated him at his right hand in the heavenly realms, far above all rule and authority, power and dominion, and every title that can be given, not only in the present age but also in the one to come. And God placed all things under his feet and appointed him to be head over everything for the church, which is his body, the fullness of him who fills everything in every way" (Eph. 1:20–23).

You cannot hope too much, envision too grandly, or anticipate beyond his competence to bless. Therefore, in this chapter, we urge you to think big. In so doing, you are simply forging practical dreams for the extension of his hands, his eyes and ears, and his willing feet into greater and greater ranges of service.

Think on things such as these.

THE CHURCH AND THE WELFARE STATE

We live in the era of the welfare state.

The church is largely responsible for the coming of the modern welfare community. The church could be largely responsible for purging welfare of its faults and problems if enough believers caught the vision.

The church brought about the welfare state in two ways:

First, as we have seen, the Word that the church proclaims demands charity and justice for the poor. As this Word has permeated at least the Western world, an alerted public conscience has demanded public welfare. The church is the parent of the welfare community.

Second, because the church did not, and perhaps in some respects could not, measure up to its own ideals not all the starving were fed, not all of the homeless were given shelter, and not all the oppressed and exploited were relieved. The cries of the needy ascended to heaven. The Lord answered with the welfare state. The government undertakes to do what the church demands and then fails to achieve by itself.

Thus, the church is, both by commission and by omission, author of the welfare state. Christians start from here. Government has undertaken to do what conscience, tutored out of the Scriptures, demands but fails, through the church, entirely to achieve.

It is futile, now, to argue long over the rights and wrongs of the welfare state. History will not reverse itself.

What is important, with an eye on tomorrow, is to discern what constructive relationships may be developed between the church and public welfare. Consider the following:

First, the Christian knows that all goods come from the hand of God. How stimulating for the needy on welfare to know that. God in heaven, looking down on distress and responding to its cry, gives. This is exactly what welfare *is*—God's giving. You know that, but are you saying it? Are you teaching critics of the welfare system that God alone provides? That he is basic to welfare, and that without his Fatherly care neither birds of the air nor man nor beast would eat at all: "Look at the birds of the air; they do not sow or reap or store away in barns, and yet your heavenly Father feeds them. Are you not much more valuable than they?"

(Matt. 6:26). God alone makes welfare possible. This must always be known and said, even though under normal circumstances both he and we prefer that bread be given from above by way of our work here below: "He who has been stealing must steal no longer, but must work, doing something useful with his own hands," says Paul, though we must not neglect what follows: "that he may have something to share with those in need" (Eph. 4:28). The needy, whom the Lord supplies through the work of others, will always be with us (John 12:8). Public welfare is one of the Lord's vehicles of provision for the needy as he also provides for the birds of the air. The needy should know this. So should the rest of us.

Second, the state, however, appears in welfare as a neutral agent. Welfare workers may or may not take an interest in pointing recipients to the original giver. This fact should burden the heart of the believer and of the church. It becomes a driving incentive for churches to get involved in the welfare system. Let God be properly honored and thanked for checks that come from the state but bear the return address of heaven. This is the basis for your interest in infiltrating the welfare process.

Third, the state has no incentive to involve churches as witnesses to the largesse of their Lord. But the state does have an interest in efficiency, and economy, and getting the most out of every welfare dollar. And here the church finds its lever. Welfare is notoriously the victim of what must be generalized regulations, made to apply to everyone and therefore applicable precisely to almost no one. Justice in the abstract, which is the only way that justice can be sought through legislation, comes in practice to be injustice, often, in the concrete. Some recipients get more, or other, than they need; some get less, even much less; while others are constantly tempted to "beat" the system in every way they can. Overburdened and usually unappreciated caseworkers struggle between bureaucracy and reality, frustrated by both. Many do heroic work against sometimes crushing odds. How much they could use the steady hand, firm faith, and constructive vision of the church. Is such a combination impossible? Forbidden by the separation of church and state? All depends on how big you are willing to dream, and to work, and to hope, and to pray. "Jesus came to them and said, 'All authority in heaven and on earth has been given to me'" (Matt. 28:18)? Your Lord, or the state? What have you asked him and trusted him to do about welfare lately? He has given you every incentive to break, somehow, into the system.

Finally, welfare, now, is commonly impersonal. Instead of creating community, it tends to destroy it. The caseworker can rarely provide the personal touch that the love of Christ incites the Christian to radiate. How much more the welfare system, just as it is, could do for uniting the needy with the rest of society if the money and the assistance were given in the name of our common God and Father. Churches could see to that, if welfare were somehow administered with your help. Even if you only went along with the caseworker and stayed behind to round out what he or she does in the neutral name of government. Have you ever thought of that? It will be probably your best chance of worming your way into an otherwise crumbling public ministry.

Yes, we think of deliberate strategies. Your goal is to restore charity to the church, which alone is fully capable of administering genuine service. Perhaps you begin by tagging along and staying to add in goods or dollars or teaching or listening or whatever love senses is lacking in the welfare program as it applies to this particular person or family. Perhaps, if you do that well, you can join other Christians already serving the Lord as professional caseworkers. And, if the Lord wills, in due season much of the welfare relief done in your parish or community is finally largely funneled through church hands. Separation of church and state? Leave that to the Lord. If your church building catches fire, the tax-supported fire department will put it out. Why? For the common good. It is the common good that bridges the gap so artificially created by—we think—a misunderstanding of the First Amendment of the U.S. Constitution. And it will be the common good that chooses the efficiency of administration of welfare funds once you have demonstrated that only by individual handling of cases can welfare dollars do the most good. Try it. And with the Lord be the rest.

Try it? Yes, in ways such as the following:

Get to know all you can—all there is to know—about public welfare in your community. If yours is a rural congregation, or one in a small community where welfare is unknown, be prepared to offer assistance to churches serving in urban areas where for some families welfare is by now a way of life.

Get to know welfare caseworkers. Some may be members of your own congregation. Some, perhaps many, will be servants of the same Lord you seek to honor. Find out how you might supplement their casework, both personally and with assistance in goods and funds.

You will no doubt discover that while welfare basically consists of "throwing money" at problems, there remains much left over for others to do. There might be cooperation with caseworkers in teaching right use of money, better ways of heating, of preparing food, of caring for household goods, and making clothes go a longer way. Cooperation between welfare workers and collections of used clothing and staple foods maintained by volunteer workers at the church opens doors.

Venture further by proposing pilot projects, in which the church undertakes to assume the welfare load for selected families for a period of time. Do this under public scrutiny with open books and preconceived measures of efficiency. Let the figures speak. Let the families testify to what the touch of love adds to the welfare dollar, and thus undertake to convince the public mind that welfare need not be a "mess," if done in his name and through his—that is, your—hands. Do you know of a better gleam of hope to shed into a system of public charity no one likes but no one knows how to amend?

Do a study of what is so readily called "the separation of church and state." Note that the First Amendment not only rejects public "establishment" (that is tax support) of religion, but equally prohibits the state from interference with "the free exercise thereof." Some day that second clause will reopen the doors of public education to Christianity. But for now let the believer observe that the so-called "wall of separation" is breached, as we have already observed, by the common good. Not only in the case of fire but also when snow clogs the city streets leading to the church—public vehicles plow them. Taxes are not collected from religious institutions. Police protect them, as does the military in time of war or riot. The common good binds church and state together. What greater contribution, now, to the common good than setting the welfare system back on its feet? Try it, and see.

Aim at the time when a certain share of welfare funds coming

into your community are gratefully funneled through the church
That this may, in the long run, oblige your congregation to join
other congregations is all the more thrilling challenge.

Dream, Christian.

Your vision will never outreach God's grasp.

THE CHURCH AND 14 INTERNATIONAL COMMUNITY

THE CHURCH OF JESUS CHRIST IS ONE

One head implies one body: "There is one body and one Spirit—just as you were called to one hope when you were called—one Lord, one faith, one baptism; one God and Father of all, who is over all and through all and in all" (Eph. 4:4–6).

The church has for centuries confessed her unity: "I believe one, holy, catholic church." So goes the Apostles Creed.

Notice that the church universal is the object of belief, not of sight: "Now faith is being sure of what we hope for and certain of what we do not see" (Heb. 11:1). "I believe one, holy, catholic church"—so millions of Christians have confessed across hundreds of years. So we join them today.

We know, however, that the church universal does become visible in the local congregation. But the visible unity of the entire church has never been achieved, and since the Reformation seems further removed than ever from accomplishment. Denominational divisions are not eclipsed by various national and international councils of churches. Nor has the breach between Protestantism and Rome ever been healed.

The visible institutional unity of the church may never be achieved. Certainly in this era it remains an object of faith. While the institutional unity of the church lags far behind our confession, a united deed witness opens a fruitful avenue to visible oneness.

Christian stewards, sacrificing themselves for the welfare of others, make visible individually the power of their faith. Viewed together, Christian stewards demonstrate the essential unity of the church, bound by that faith.

The oneness of the church becomes even more apparent in co-operative service rendered by countless ministries. Believers should push for such evidence of the church's unity.

The church has but one Savior, Head, Master, Lord. And because this is so, the church is, in his holy sight, one body. Therefore, Christian stewards are always his hands, no matter from which congregation they extend mercy. Christian stewards are always his eyes, no matter where opened to need. Christian stewards are always his ears, whatever and wherever the cries they discern. Christian stewards bent on his errands are ever his feet no matter from where and to whom they hasten.

Remember this, believers.

Yours is the overt and visible testimony to the unity of the body of Christ. When your service is joined with that of others, you make still more visible the oneness of the church. All who lift their eyes to regional, national, and even international stewardship aspire to ever more visible witness to the one, holy, catholic church. Stewardship pursued cooperatively becomes visible sinew binding the universal church into objective unity.

Take inspiration from reflecting that the church is the most enduring and most comprehensive of all institutions. No institution has lived longer and broken through more barriers of language, culture, and geography than has the church. How better, then, to manifest this universal and enduring body than in united witness by deed?

SUMMARY

Every Christian should use whatever gift he has received to serve others, faithfully administering God's grace in its various forms. If anyone speaks, he should do it as one speaking the very words of God. If anyone serves, he should do it with the strength God provides, so that in all things God may be praised through Jesus Christ. To him be the glory and the power forever and ever. Amen.

—1 Peter 4:10–11

Life, time, talent and all that each of us has are gifts of God. The right stewardship of all these gifts is what life is for.

The textbook to right stewardship is the Bible.

The school for instruction in the Bible is the church.

The priesthood of all believers works through self-sacrifice to present to God the fruits of obedient stewardship.

That is what this book has been all about.

EPILOG

I will sing for the one I love
    a song about his vineyard:
My loved one had a vineyard
    on a fertile hillside.

He dug it up and cleared it of stones
    and planted it with the choicest vines.
He built a watchtower in it
    and cut out a winepress as well.
Then he looked for a crop of good grapes,
    but it yielded only bad fruit.

                  —Isa. 5:1–2

He is still looking to the church and to you,
Christian steward, whoever and wherever you are.

NIV STEWARDSHIP STUDY BIBLE

The *NIV Stewardship Study Bible* was created as a companion to your journey toward becoming a mature and effective steward. Through the use of reflective meditations and study notes tied to Scripture and organized around stewardship messages, this Bible will encourage your growth and provide rich biblical and theological resources to draw you more deeply into the stewardship teachings of God's Word.

Stewardship is not just about what we do; it is ultimately about who God is and what he desires us to become. Effective, biblical stewardship is not like a destination on a map, it is more like a journey. We invite you to explore God's plans for you as his manager in trust through this Bible.

The common theme in every feature of this Bible illustrates the challenge and the promise found in Matthew 25:23: "You have been faithful with a few things; I will put you in charge of many things."

For more information, visit
STORE.ACTON.ORG.

OUR GREAT EXCHANGE

Why would an all knowing God call us to be stewards of his creation? Why were we granted such a high calling as his stewards? In God's economy, we play a profound role. With the help of our guide, Jim Liske, CEO of Prison Fellowship Ministries, the *Our Great Exchange* small group video study features inspiring stories and key biblical insights. The seven-session series takes us on a journey to explore his purposes for our stewardship of all he created.

These powerful small group videos will spark valuable discussion in your group. In addition to the videos, the series includes a study guide and leader's guide, over 75 minutes of bonus video, Bible passages, and supplemental content from the *NIV Stewardship Study Bible*, all available on the electronic device of your choice at StudySpace.org. The Study Space site allows your group to stay connected to the content and to each other throughout the study—any time, any place, any device.

For more information, visit
OURGREATEXCHANGE.COM.

ABOUT THE AUTHORS

GERARD BERGHOEF (1926–2007) was a native of the Netherlands, who emigrated to the United States early in the 1950s. He worked as a furniture manufacturing executive and served the Christian Reformed Church as an elder.

LESTER DEKOSTER (1916–2009) became director of the library at Calvin College and Seminary, affiliated with the Christian Reformed Church in North America, in 1951. He earned his doctorate from the University of Michigan in 1964, after completing a dissertation on "Living Themes in the Thought of John Calvin: A Bibliographical Study." During his tenure at the college, DeKoster was influential in expanding the holdings of what would become the H. Henry Meeter Center for Calvin Studies, one of the preeminent collections of Calvinist and Reformed texts in the world. DeKoster also amassed an impressive personal library of some ten thousand books, which includes a wide array of sources testifying to both the breadth and depth of his intellectual vigor.

DeKoster was a professor of speech at the college and enjoyed taking up the part of historic Christianity and confessional Reformed theology in debates on doctrinal and social issues that pressed the church throughout the following decades. Both his public debates and private correspondence were marked by a spirit of charity that tempered and directed the needed words of rebuke. After his retirement from Calvin College in 1969, DeKoster labored for a decade as the editor of *The Banner*, the denominational magazine of the Christian Reformed Church. This position provided him with another platform from which to critically engage the life of the church and the world. During this time DeKoster also launched, in collaboration with Gerard Berghoef (a longtime elder in the church) and their families, the Christian's Library Press, a publishing endeavor intended to provide timely resources both for the church's laity and its leadership.

BRETT A. ELDER serves as the director of collaborative initiatives at Acton Institute, where he produces rich media resources, small group curricula, and creative digital delivery platforms. Brett has a lifetime commitment to exploring the intersection of faith, freedom, and virtue in the context of God's economy of all things. This pursuit prompted the founding of the Stewardship Council where Brett continues to serve as the executive director as well as the executive editor of the council's seminal resource, the *NIV Stewardship Study Bible*. Brett also serves as an advisor of International Steward, a ministry dedicated to encouraging mature stewardship in the emerging church around the world. A graduate of Western Michigan University, Brett served as Director of Finance and Administration for the Acton Institute for the Study of Religion and Liberty for five years prior to helping launch the ministry of International Steward in 2000.